Contents

Ethical eye

Euthanasia

Volume II – National and European perspectives

French version:

Regard éthique – L'Euthanasie
Volume II – Perspectives nationales et européennes
ISBN 92-871-5199-7

Cover photo: Christophe Hamm
Cover design: Graphic Design Workshop, Council of Europe
Layout: Desktop Publishing Unit, Council of Europe

Edited by Council of Europe Publishing
http://book.coe.int

Council of Europe Publishing
F-67075 Strasbourg Cedex

ISBN 92-871-5200-4
© Council of Europe, January 2004
Printed in Germany

Contributors

Yvon Englert

Doctor of medicine, Yvon Englert also holds a post-doctoral qualification from the Free University of Brussels *(agrégation de l'enseignement supérieur)* in gynaecological and obstetrical sciences. He has done a considerable amount of lecturing and research, especially relating to fertility. He is a member of the Council of Europe's COMETH (European Conference of National Ethics Committees) and of the European Commission's European Group on Ethics in Science and New Technologies, and was Chairperson of the Belgian Committee on Bioethics and, until 2001, an expert on the Council of Europe's Steering Committee on Bioethics. Since 2002, he has been head of the Gynaecology/Obstetrics Department of the Hôpital Erasme and head of the Human Reproduction Research Laboratory at the Free University of Brussels.

Jørn Vestergaard

Jørn Vestergaard, Ph.D., is associate professor of Criminal Law at University of Copenhagen. Having published extensively within the fields of criminal law and health law, he is Director of the Research section III at the Faculty of Law (www.jur.ku.dk/retd). As a member of the Danish Council of Ethics and Chairperson of the council's Working Group on Euthanasia, he was responsible for drafting the major 1997 report on euthanasia. In addition, he has written several articles on the legal aspects of euthanasia.

Givi Javashvili

Having graduated from Tbilisi State Medical University, Givi Javashvili (MD, Ph.D.) is now expert-consultant in the Department of Health Law and Bioethics at the National Institute of Health and Vice-Chairperson of the National Council on Bioethics. He is also Chairman of the Georgian Health Law and Bioethics Society (since 1998) and Georgia's representative on the Council of Europe's Steering Committee on Bioethics (CDBI) and has been a member of the CDBI Bureau since 2002.

Guram Kiknadze

Guram Kiknadze is currently head of the Department of Health Law and Bioethics at the National Institute of Health, Co-Chairperson of the Georgian Health Law and Bioethics Society and Professor of Clinical Medicine at Tbilisi State Medical Academy of Postgraduate Medical Training.

Bela Blasszauer

Bela Blasszauer was born in Budapest, Hungary, and is a lawyer and specialist in medical sciences. For more than twenty years he worked as a teacher of medical ethics at the Institute of Behavioural Sciences, Medical University of Pecs, and is now a scientific adviser to the Institute of Family Medicine at the University of Pecs. He has written widely and his first textbook on medical ethics, now in its second edition, is used by most Hungarian medical faculties and health institutes.

Johannes van Delden

Professor Johannes van Delden holds the Chair in Medical Ethics at the Julius Centre for Health Sciences and Primary Care, University Medical Centre, Utrecht (Netherlands). He is also a practising physician, working at the Rosendael nursing home in Utrecht. He was one of the principal architects of the first nationwide study on euthanasia and other medical decisions concerning the end of life, and has published widely on these issues. He serves as an ethicist on one of the five assessment committees for euthanasia.

Daniel Serrão

Professor of Pathological Anatomy until 1998, Daniel Serrão is currently Professor of Bioethics and Medical Ethics at the Faculty of Medicine, University of Oporto, where he teaches to master's degree level. A member of the National Ethics Committee for Life Sciences and Chairperson of the Ethical Council of the Order of Doctors, he also chairs the Health Ministry's Committee for the Development of Health Care Research, as well as being on the National Oncology Commission. He is

Portugal's representative on the Council of Europe's Steering Committee on Bioethics.

Alberto Bondolfi

Alberto Bondolfi studied philosophy and theology at the University of Fribourg (Switzerland), and obtained a doctorate in theological ethics in 1977. After spending many years as a research worker and teacher at the Institut für Sozialethik, University of Zurich, he was appointed Professor of Ethics at the Centre Lémanique d'Ethique, University of Lausanne. He is also a member of the National Ethics Committee of the Swiss Confederation and a former President of Societas Ethica, the European Society for Research in Ethics. He has written numerous publications in the field of biomedical ethics.

Sheila McLean

International Bar Association Professor of Law and Ethics in Medicine, and Director of the Institute of Law and Ethics in Medicine at the University of Glasgow, Sheila McLean was the founding Chairperson of the Scottish Criminal Cases Review Commission and the Inter-Agency Forum on Female Offending. She also serves on a number of national and international committees, as well as on the editorial board of national and international journals. She has written numerous books and articles.

Lois Snyder

Lois Snyder is Director of the Centre for Ethics and Professionalism at the American College of Physicians, the national professional society of doctors of internal medicine and the sub-specialties of internal medicine. She is also Adjunct Assistant Professor of Bioethics and Fellow of the University of Pennsylvania Centre for Bioethics. She joined the College in 1987 and Penn in 1994 after serving as a health care consultant on medical malpractice and bioethics issues for hospitals. Lois received her BA in Health Planning and Policy from the University of Pennsylvania and her law degree from the evening division of the Temple University School of Law. She is a frequent writer and speaker on health care policy, bioethical and medical legal issues. She has edited a number of books, including *The physician's guide to end-of-life care and ethical choices: case studies for medical practice.*

Dick Marty

Dick Marty, a Doctor of Law, worked with the Max Planck Institute (Freiburg im Brisgau) on research into comparative criminal law and criminology before serving for fifteen years as a prosecution magistrate. He was then elected member of the government of Ticino canton for six years and for the past eight years has been a member of the Swiss Council of States (Senate). As representative to the Council of Europe Parliamentary Assembly, he is First Vice-Chair of its Legal Affairs Committee and also belongs to its Social, Health and Family Affairs Committee.

Elaine Gadd

Elaine Gadd is a qualified doctor and former Chairperson of the Council of Europe's Steering Committee on Bioethics. She is presently on secondment to the Council of Europe's Bioethics Department from the Department of Health, England.

Piotr Mierzewski

MD, Piotr Mierzewski has worked in the Health Division (Social Cohesion) of the Council of Europe since 1994. He first studied and then lectured at the Medical University of Gdańsk, Poland. He served as the First Deputy Minister of Health in the first non-communist government in Poland (1989-92), then became Director of the National Centre for Health System Management, Warsaw. Recently he has served as a Secretary of the Committee of Experts on the Organisation of Palliative care, which prepared a draft recommendation adopted by the Council of Europe Committee of Ministers.

Preface

by Walter Schwimmer
Secretary General of the Council of Europe

The fourth book in the "Ethical eye" series focuses on euthanasia, a subject that has been widely discussed across Europe. We all have to face the prospect of death, and how that should be managed arouses our deepest personal feelings as well as engaging the most profound moral and theological beliefs. It is not surprising therefore that the question of euthanasia is passionately debated, and that different individuals, and different states, have reached different conclusions on this issue.

This book does not aim to provide a definitive answer to the question of euthanasia. Rather, it aims to contribute to the political and public debates on this issue by drawing together reflections on the range of ethical and human dimensions that are relevant to the question (Volume I) and reviewing the position both at the European level and in a number of different countries (Volume II). These reviews illustrate the different legal approaches to issues relevant to euthanasia that are in place at present, including refusal of or withdrawing treatment, assisted suicide, and active interventions to end life. The review of the work of the Parliamentary Assembly shows that these issues remain under active consideration by parliamentarians as well as by the wider public.

As was shown in the Council of Europe's survey of the law and practice of member states in this field, which is also reviewed in this book, there is no single agreed definition of "euthanasia". Therefore, this book takes a wide perspective on medical decision-making at the end of life. In that context, it is clear that there is already a consensus on the value and importance of palliative care at the end of life, even whilst other aspects of end-of-life decision-making remain actively under debate.

The importance of these issues is acknowledged by all, and it is my hope that this book will contribute to the continuing reflections on this issue at both the national and the European level.

Euthanasia in Europe and the United States

Belgium – Evolution of the debate

by Yvon Englert

Did the Speakers of the upper and lower houses of the Belgian Parliament realise in 1996, when they asked the recently formed Consultative Committee on Bioethics to look into euthanasia and parliamentary bills pending on the subject, that this was to be the trigger for a society-wide debate of remarkably high quality and an intensity hitherto unmatched in Belgium? Whatever the answer, it is reasonable to see this moment as marking the public emergence of a radical shift in Christian thinking. For there is no doubt that it was the public stances by several eminent people, including members of the Church, acknowledging the real demand for euthanasia, that allowed the debate to take place. From that point on, the public became intensely involved, as previous excuses for avoiding debate – the claim that euthanasia was requested only in exceptional and extremely rare cases, or that palliative care was a universal solution, and reference to the medical profession's ethical prohibition on taking life – gave way one after another. Admittedly, there was some prevarication but the real question was eventually tabled: Given that a demand for euthanasia existed, was it, in principle, ethically legitimate to respond to it? Society, through parliament, answered the question with a cautious "Yes, but ..." and laid down specific procedures, contexts and limits subject to which doctors were allowed to respond. Naturally, conflict and disagreement persisted: some people feared the implications of officially recognising an action which, despite its underlying compassion and supportiveness, they equated with murder; others were reluctant to place such a premium on patient autonomy and gave precedence neither to social control nor medical authority.

A particular feature of the debate was the confusion between two distinct concepts: legality on the one hand and medical good practice on the other. The Belgian Parliament's desire for legal certainty in euthanasia meant stipulating the circumstances in which a person who helped a patient to die would not face charges. This was a question of both substance (what type of euthanasia could be legal) and form (what procedures would have to be followed). But the debate was often complicated by an apparent wish to lay down what constituted good medical practice – as if a request for euthanasia could take only one form and there was only one way for doctors to interpret and acknowledge it, manage it and respond to it. This led to pointless confrontation, denying the particular interpersonal context and the infinite range of actual human situations that characterise all therapeutic relationships and most certainly the intense relationships formed in the days before a death. Seeking to control such relationships inevitably means stereotyping and sterilising them, substituting the legislator for the carer and, in the process, denying the carer's special role and responsibilities. A feature of the debate, right throughout the legislative process, was an openness on all sides to the views of others, with mutual respect for what were sometimes quite divergent positions and a general recognition that we could continue to co-exist while holding different opinions on those two crucial moments of existence, conception and death. Parliament's role was to establish a framework broad enough to accommodate the sensitivities of different sections of the population while affording people a freedom of action that would allow them the least distressful death possible. Once such a framework is in place, it is up to the medical profession, through practice and exchanges of experience, to develop the various approaches to care and support for the dying.

In any event, it is already clear that the ethical debate in Belgian society over the last six years has led to the forging of new links and helped people to familiarise themselves with ideas different from their own. It is to be hoped that it marks a turning point in the history of ethical debate in Belgium: such debate used to split our society but this time we seem to be moving towards a new model of pluralism that will help social cohesion by promoting respect for differences.

Background

Although the ethical debate about euthanasia goes back a very long way (the fact that Hippocrates felt the need to prohibit euthanasia in his oath implies that doctors were breaking the prohibition even then), the social debate in Belgium really came into focus when, in 1996, the Speakers of both the Chamber of Representatives and the Senate asked the recently formed Consultative Committee on Bioethics to give its opinion on the advisability of legislating on ending of life at the request of the terminally ill (that is, euthanasia); palliative care; "living wills"; and the bills on these subjects then before parliament.

It was an exceptional step (and one that has not been repeated since) for the Speakers of both houses to approach the committee jointly in this way. Was it a sign that debate had attained a degree of maturity, or was it a delaying tactic or, indeed, an early test for the consultative committee, which some commentators had already written off in advance? It may have been all these things. In any case, on 12 May 1997, the committee delivered to the two Speakers an initial opinion on the advisability of statutory provision with regard to euthanasia.[1] In December of that year, the Senate invited the authors of the report to take part in two days of public discussion, which marked the beginning of the debate both in civil society and among politicians.

In early 1999 the committee delivered a second opinion on active termination of the lives of persons incapable of expressing their wishes,[2] addressing the question of whether prior instructions given by the patient could be regarded as legitimate, as well as the role of patients' representatives and situations where patients could not or did not issue prior instructions. This opinion ranged well beyond the issue of the patient's will, taking in artificial prolongation of life and withdrawal of treatment.

During the next parliament (1998-2002), the debate sharpened when new bills were tabled, and particularly when they came up for scrutiny by the justice and health committees. It also took a dramatic turn when several cases hit the headlines: two doctors from the Citadelle regional hospital in Liège were remanded in custody, as were a nurse and members of her family in Antwerp; and in the summer of 2001, the death by euthanasia of a terminally ill patient who had publicly explained his situation was shown practically live on a French-speaking television channel; this patient had written a book on

1.
Original title of the opinion: Avis n° 1 du Comité consultatif de bioéthique de Belgique du 12 mai 1997 concernant l'opportunité d'un règlement légal de l'euthanasie: www.health.fgov.be/bioet/fr/avis/avis-index.htm.

2.
Original title of the opinion: Avis n° 9 du Comité consultatif de bioéthique de Belgique du 22 février 1999 relatif à l'arrêt actif de la vie des personnes incapables d'exprimer leur volonté: www.health.fgov.be/bioeth/fr/avis/avis-index.htm.

the subject and had called on the Senate to decriminalise the practice. Debate on the subject was also taking off in other countries, including Italy, and in the summer of 2001 came the announcement of the death by euthanasia of a terminally ill patient who had publicly explained his situation, had written a book and had called on the Senate to decriminalise the practice. Debate on the subject was also taking off in other countries, including Italy, Switzerland and France, and was continuing in the Netherlands, to consider only Belgium's closer neighbours. Controversy about "the right way to die" had thus become a fact of society.

How the social debate developed: from recognising euthanasia in ethical terms to ending denial that it took place

For a long time, debate about the legitimacy of euthanasia was avoided as traditional views were repeated: that it was requested extremely rarely, that palliative care offered a complete answer, or that requests for euthanasia had to be "decoded", that is reinterpreted within frames of reference that ruled it out as a matter of principle. Arguably all this was an attempt to prevent the real question being addressed. However, once the Consultative Committee on Bioethics had stated that assisted death could be ethically defensible in the case of a terminally ill patient who had requested it, the debate opened up and very quickly, perhaps surprisingly so, the legitimacy "in principle" of euthanasia was to be recognised, although no decisions were yet taken on how it might be introduced as a social reality. In Belgium, another important document, apart from the opinion of the Consultative Committee on Bioethics, was the opinion, delivered on 15 January 2000, of the National Council of the Belgian Medical Association:[1]

1.
Opinion of the National Council of the Order of Doctors, 15 January 2000: www.ordomedic.be/fr /a87/a087001f.htm.

"The National Council accepts that in exceptional circumstances doctors may find themselves facing a conflict of values and value-based decisions: whether to hold back from bringing death about deliberately or to use sufficient necessary means to allow a patient to die with dignity. In such circumstances, doctors must, in consultation with the patient, take an honourable and conscientious decision which they must at any time be able to justify. We would note that in recent decades no doctors have had criminal or disciplinary proceedings brought against them for ending a patient's life, despite admissions by doctors that they have administered euthanasia on more than one occasion."

Despite the somewhat convoluted presentation, it is important to note that this further opinion was the first acknowledgment (albeit a grudging one) by the Medical Association that euthanasia might be ethically permissible. A clearer statement, and one that was at least as important symbolically, came on 31 January 2000 with publication of a joint document by the Rector of the Catholic University of Louvain and the head doctors at the university hospitals of St Luc and UCL Mont-Godinne, which included the following:

> "The culture of continuing care provides an immediate solution to the problem of prolonging life by artificial means. It implies that suffering from which there is no escape, and which defies all forms of treatment, must be identified and addressed. In this the care teams must be trusted and allowed, should their efforts fail, to assist the end of life by medical means if such remains the wish of the patient."[1].

In its Opinion No. 63, of 27 January 2000, the French Consultative Committee for Life Sciences and Health argued for the introduction of a "euthanasia exception", asserting:

> "If, in a real situation, the decision to terminate a life may, at a pinch, seem acceptable, it is not an action that has any clear and obvious ethical basis."[2]

All these bodies – traditionally more than reluctant to allow that euthanasia might be ethical – were suddenly adopting positions that reflected a considerable shift, and one apparent also in the political world for, with the exception of the extreme right, no party now argued against euthanasia's legitimacy in principle: the Belgian Catholic parties (the PSC and the CVP), while opposing decriminalisation, no longer formally condemned the act of euthanasia. In a party document entitled "Euthanasia: our view", the PSC stated:

> "Although we reject any change in the Criminal Code provision that prohibits killing, we can none the less envisage the

1.
Document on the end of life, compiled by the authorities of the Catholic University of Louvain, 31 January 2000.

2.
Original title: "Comité consultatif français pour les sciences de la vie et de la santé, Avis n° 63 du 27 janvier 2000": www.ccne-ethique.org

possibility of doctors finding themselves in, legally, a situation of necessity in which they may respond to a request for euthanasia."[1]

It is my personal interpretation that this acceleration in the pace of change can be credited to the Christian community, which saw here a practical issue relevant to advances in its ethical positions. It was this development that permitted the real public debate which began in 1997, a genuine society-wide exchange of views which has already wrought a profound change in the way that people in many caring institutions relate to the end of life. Of course there are still disagreements as deeply entrenched between the secular and Christian currents in Belgian society, but they are now about how society should handle a reality, and we have moved beyond the stage of denial that made all debate a non-starter.

Meanwhile research in Belgium (Mortier et al., 2000; Deliens et al., 2000) has demonstrated that doctors actively intervene at the end of life in roughly the same proportion of cases as in the Netherlands, namely in 4-5% of deaths. This is scarcely surprising given that the two countries' populations have a similar age structure, similar patterns of mortality and similar standards of health care. The claim that euthanasia is an exceptional problem has collapsed in the face of facts.

The argument that palliative care is the answer, rendering the question of euthanasia meaningless, has been similarly undermined. At a conference in Brussels in December 1997, organised by the Belgian Palliative Care Association, Doctor Zylicz, from the Netherlands, who opposed the practice of euthanasia in his own country and promoted palliative care, admitted that 30% of the patients admitted to his establishment requested euthanasia and that 5% of these "resisted" proper treatment of pain with morphine and of depression with anti-depressants. Doctor Zylicz further acknowledged that patients who were in favour of euthanasia did not come to his establishment. The public discussion session queried certain palliative-care practices and, for the first time, "insistence on palliative care" was mentioned as a possible danger. Debate of this kind is not something practitioners of palliative care can ignore, because it raises real issues: the whole question of sedation, for example,

1.
Euthanasie, ce que nous pensons, publication of the PSC, 2000.

which is undoubtedly the most controversial palliative-care practice. There have also been claims – against all the evidence of surveys – that the medical profession is massively opposed to decriminalisation. Publication, while the issue was being debated in parliament, of a list of 2 400 doctors who supported the clearly worded decriminalisation bill tabled by six MPs of the Rainbow majority put an end to this red herring: the medical world, like society generally, is split on the legalities of an issue in which they find themselves highly vulnerable, but many of them are prepared to incur heavy responsibility – and some are already doing so – in an extremely thorny area. It is fair to say that the social debate ceased to be about euthanasia as such, because only a small fringe of society really continued to dispute its legitimacy in principle.

What were the expectations of those who favoured partial decriminalisation?

Pending adoption of a new law, all euthanasia was classified as murder. Yet it was no secret that euthanasia was practised in Belgium both in hospitals and homes and that only exceptionally did the law step in. From a pragmatic point of view, disregarding the rule of law, there was a case for leaving things as they were. Some members of the medical profession supported this line. However, breaking the law is breaking the law, and carries a risk of prosecution. Legal uncertainty of that kind is incompatible with healthily functioning democracy.

Because practice of euthanasia is clandestine or semi-clandestine, patients are denied treatment in accordance with their convictions. In 1998 the Belgian television programme "Ecran témoin" (Witness) gave a telling illustration. Madame Urbain's husband had pleaded with his doctor to end his suffering. The doctor, who appeared on the programme, acknowledged in all frankness that the patient ought to have been helped to die. Madame Urbain explained that, as a mother with family responsibilities, she had not dared, or been able, to put her job and freedom at risk by suggesting a step so fraught with legal consequences.

It is also the case that, in order to avoid a distressing dilemma, many doctors tend either to turn a deaf ear to requests that are more or less clearly expressed, or to reply in ambiguous terms. Some even choose to offer false hope of improvement, thus distorting the doctor-patient relationship at a time when it is particularly important.

All types of medical practice have to be taught, and experience gained and passed on is a key factor in progressing towards the best possible standard of health care. But in a context of blanket prohibition it is impossible for the medical world to debate fundamental aspects of the euthanasia question. In what situations must a request for euthanasia be given a hearing, and how can the listening function in the doctor-patient relationship be developed to ensure that such requests are correctly interpreted? It has to be established whether the request is genuinely a call for life to be ended or whether it is a call for help by a person who still wants to live. Is the patient suffering from a transient bout of depression, or does the request reflect a considered decision? The law can never provide answers to such questions, but it can afford people the scope to speak freely, thus giving practitioners the time and space they need to assume what is a heavy responsibility that goes with their caring function. Efforts to achieve a statutory definition of professional standards, while tempting, are mistaken, they represent a distortion of the law-maker's role and, last but not least, they are doomed to failure.

However – and it is one of the most perverse effects of criminalisation – even when euthanasia occurs it cannot be practised in the climate of openness and directness that is called for: a doctor who takes on board a patient's request is unable to speak freely about it with the patient, and may end up carrying out the patient's wishes without actually telling the patient in so many words. This strips the act of euthanasia of an important philosophical dimension – the patient's right to experience and reassert ownership of his or her death. And doctors are not the only ones affected. A study carried out among intensive care nurses in the United States and published in the respected *New England Journal of Medicine* (Asch, 1996) reveals that, in a context much more repressive than that existing in Belgium, nurses too are willing to take on full responsibility. Of 827 nurses questioned, 15% (one in six) admitted that in the course of their careers they had terminated a life on at least one occasion. Even more surprising was the finding that in a third of such cases, the nurse was not acting at a doctor's request. While we may salute their courage, there are grounds here for concern about situations that demonstrate illegality's perverse effects on inter-carer relationships.

Finally, we have referred to the heavy responsibility that ending a life represents for carers generally and for doctors in particular. Having to take such a decision leaves a lasting psychological mark, whether the doctor accedes to the patient's request or not. Doctors, too, need to be able to talk about such experiences and receive support if they are not to find themselves suffering from "burnout" – but where secrecy prevails talking is impossible.

Those in favour of decriminalisation therefore sought to create a frame of legal certainty in which doctors who honestly felt the need to broach the subject of euthanasia with a patient, or indeed to practise euthanasia, could do so without fear of breaking the law provided that strict criteria were met.

Such a framework is necessary not only for doctors but also for patients, so that they can discuss the issue with their doctors, if only to be reassured that the doctor will be there when the patient decides that his or her presence is vital. Many patients in the Netherlands need to have this space in which to talk and the great majority of them, knowing that it is available, will never request euthanasia. The most striking effect of making euthanasia "official" in 1990 was that it allowed a great many patients to discuss the subject with their doctors (Van der Maas et al., 1996). To steer the debate onto end-of-life situations in the intensive care unit is to avoid the issue: the great majority of patients in intensive care are *de facto* incapable, and quite different questions then arise. It is also worth bearing in mind that the great majority of us will not die in intensive care.

Decriminalisation of euthanasia is also a logical step from the point of view of patients' rights, another subject on which legislation has been passed,[1] for it entails transferring the decision-making power from the doctor to the patient, and legislation would seem the right way to achieve this in a state governed by the rule of law. For some people, however, it is a difficult step to take, indeed an insurmountable barrier in symbolic terms.

Belgium's Euthanasia Act of 28 May 2002 lays down the conditions under which a doctor may practise euthanasia without breaking the law. The key section of the act sets out criteria very similar to those used in the Netherlands:

– that the patient be adult and conscious;

– that the request be made of the patient's own volition, after reflection, and be repeated;

– that there be no medical solution to the situation;

– that the patient be experiencing constant, unbearable physical or mental suffering that cannot be relieved;

– that the patient's condition as a result of accident or illness be serious and incurable.

The procedure to be followed by the doctor entails:

– supplying the patient with information;

– confirming the persistence of the symptoms and of the patient's wish;

– consulting a second doctor;

– consulting the care team and, if the patient so wishes, other parties.

The law stipulates that a time-scale be observed, that the procedure be documented in the patient's file and that a declaration be submitted to a federal commission whose tasks are to ensure that procedure is properly followed, to compile annual statistics for parliament, and to forward to the Office of Public Prosecutions any declarations pertaining to cases where it suspects the statutory conditions have not been observed. There is further provision, however, for any citizen of adult years, in possession of his or her faculties, to draw up a prior declaration (valid for five years and renewable) requesting euthanasia

1.
See the website 94.7.188.126/justice/index_fr.htm, loi relative aux droits du patient (Patient's Rights Act), 22 August 2002.

2.
See the website 194.7.188.126/justice/index_fr.htm, loi relative à l'euthanasie (Euthanasia Act), 28 May 2002.

in the event of unconsciousness that, to the best of current medical knowledge, is not reversible. Those who draw up such declarations may also designate one or more representatives to inform the doctor responsible of the unconscious patient's wishes. This provision should be seen alongside the Patient's Rights Act, a more general piece of legislation on the rights and duties of medical practitioners in relation to patients, in which patients' representatives play an even broader role inasmuch as they step in to exercise rights that the patient cannot exercise for himself or herself due to incapacity, whether temporary or permanent. Under the new law, assessments about the options of artificially prolonging life or terminating treatment will no longer be made by the medical team alone but will first be discussed with the patient's representative (if such a person has been appointed), who will have real legal authority to exercise the rights of the unconscious patient.

Belgian society is divided on euthanasia and, as in other difficult ethical debates, certain divisions cannot be overcome. What society has to do is not to decide who is right and who is wrong, but rather to find a way in which different ethical visions can co-exist. In a truly pluralistic society, it might have been hoped that even those opposed to decriminalisation would support it because they respected the values of others.

It is to be hoped that decriminalisation will improve interpersonal relations at what is a key moment in human existence: for some, a return to the void; for others, a rite of passage. Allowing people to speak freely, granting patients their rights, allowing the act of assisting death – which must be a compassionate and humane act – to be carried out in a context of clarity: these are the issues.

I am convinced that this change in the law will not make killing a commonplace occurrence. On the contrary, it will strip dubious practices of any legitimacy, reduce the incidence of euthanasia not at the patient's request, and help people to take the very necessary step of reappropriating their own deaths.

References

Asch, D.A., "The role of critical care nurses in euthanasia and assisted suicide", *NEJM*, 334 (21), 23 May 1996, pp. 1374-1379.

Deliens, L., Mortier, F., Bilsen, J., Cosyns, M., van der Stichele, R., Vanoverloop, J. and Ingels, K., "End-of-life decisions in medical practice in Flanders, Belgium: a nationwide survey", *Lancet*, 356 (9244), 25 November 2000, pp. 1806-1811.

Mortier, F., Deliens, L., Bilsen, J., Cosyns, M., Ingels, K. and van der Stichele, R., "End-of-life decisions of physicians in the city of Hasselt (Belgium)", *Bioethics*, 14 (3), July 2000, pp. 254-267.

Van der Maas, P.J., van der Wal, G., Haverkate, I., de Graaff, C.L., Kester, J.G., Onwuteaka-Philipsen, B.D., van der Heide, A., Bosma, J.M. and Willems, D.L., "Euthanasia, physician-assisted suicide, and other medical practices involving the end of life in the Netherlands, 1990-1995", *NEJM*, 335 (22), 28 November 1996, pp. 1699-1705.

Denmark – The right to self-determination

by Jørn Vestergaard[1]

Under Danish law,[2] substantial weight should always be attached to a principle of making the last part of the patient's life as good as possible, whether or not the patient is capable of exercising a right to self-determination.[3] The right to passive euthanasia is fully recognised.

This, of course, has a major clinical impact in relation to renouncing life-prolonging treatment of terminally ill patients and to the initiation of alleviating treatment which might slightly accelerate the moment of death. However, active euthanasia in the form of killing on request or assisted suicide is a criminal offence.

The background for the legal provisions on patients' self-determination

In 1976 the Danish National Association "My Living Will – The Right to a Dignified Death"[4] was established. Approximately 25 000 members filed living wills on the association's standard formula. However, the legal status of such an advance directive was uncertain.

During the same period of time, the National Board of Health dissociated itself from the notion that a physician should always be under an obligation to make every possible endeavour to preserve life. To that effect, the National Board of Health announced in 1974 in a press release that it is not in violation of "commonly recognised principles for good medical practice that the responsible physician decides to abstain from initiating or continuing measures that could only defer the moment of death". The National Board of Health also stated that when treatment of the patient is futile and death is imminent, it is "justified to administer the necessary analgesic remedies, even though this as an unpremeditated effect might invoke a risk that death occurs slightly earlier", a statement which officially justified the double effect.

1.
The author has been a member of the Danish Council of Ethics for five years. As Chairperson of a working group under the council, he drafted *Medical aid in dying? A Report*, Copenhagen, 1996.

2.
For a more extensive account in Danish law of the various aspects regarding medical aid in dying, see the author's article in *European Journal of Health Law*, 7, 2000, pp. 405-425.

3.
The 1996 report on aid in dying *(Dødshjælp)* by the Danish Council of Ethics includes an elaborate section on palliation in Chapter 4. In 1996, the National Board of Health issued a set of professional guidelines concerning palliative measures. A revised edition appeared in 1999.

4.
Landsforeningen mit livstestamente – Retten til en værdig død.

Moreover, in 1976, the Director General of the National Board of Health stated to the press that a living will might well be assigned relevance, as a physician could take such an advance directive into consideration along with a number of other factors, when the difficult decision had to be taken at the end of life. From a prosecutor's perspective, the Attorney General endorsed that a living will might be included as one of many elements in the exercise of justified medical discretion.

For years, the National Association "My Living Will" requested a legal recognition of living wills. In 1992 a set of provisions on aid in dying was enacted as amendments to the Physicians' Act, after which the National Association "My Living Will" dissolved, as its mission was conceived to have been successfully completed.

In 1996, the Danish Council of Ethics issued a major report concerning aid in dying, including a set of recommendations.[1]

Originally, the statutory provisions on informed consent and aid in dying were amended to the Physicians' Act. In 1998, they were clarified and moved to a new, comprehensive Patients' Rights Act which regulates the general principles concerning the relation between patient and health care professional in regard of self-determination and access to information. In the following, the act will be referred to as the PRA.[2]

Renouncing treatment

Competent patients

The patient's right to self-determination – The rules concerning informed consent

The fundamental principle concerning the patient's right to self-determination was initially demonstrated in 1976 in an administrative circular issued by the National Board of Health and later codified in statutory provisions in 1992.

A patient's right to self-determination should normally be respected if the concerned party is a person older than 15 years, who from a legal perspective is mentally competent, so that he or she is sufficiently able to understand and assess the

1.
A summary in English has been published in the Council of Bioethics' annual report.

2.
The statutory provisions are supplemented by a number of administrative regulations. The Ministry of Health has issued governmental Order No. 663/1998 on living wills. Under this order, the National Board of Health has issued administrative Regulation No. 482/1998 and Guidelines No. 158/1998 concerning physicians' duties regarding living wills. Furthermore, the Ministry of Health has issued governmental Order No. 665 on informed consent. Regarding informed consent, the National Board of Health has issued administrative Guidelines No. 161/1998. Finally, the National Board of Health has issued administrative guidelines on morphine drip.

situation. Normally, such a patient should not be subject to any kind of involuntary commitment or treatment, including life-prolonging treatment. Exceptions to this principle require a statutory authorisation, which exists only under the Penal Code, the Mental Health Care Act and the Epidemic Disease Act.

The rules were clarified in 1998 in connection with the enactment of a new comprehensive code on patients' rights.[1] The first article of the PRA states the basic objective regarding promotion of respect for patients' dignity, integrity and right to self-determination, and of confidence and confidentiality in the relation between patient and health care professional.

"The aim of this act is to ensure that patients' dignity, integrity and right to self-determination be respected. Furthermore, the act shall contribute to ensure confidence and confidentiality in the relation between patient and health care professional."[2]

The provisions concerning informed consent are now to be found in the PRA, Articles 6 and 7.

"Article 6

No treatment may be initiated or continued without the patient's informed consent, unless otherwise stated by law [...].

6.2. At any time, the patient may revoke prior consent under the first paragraph of this article.

6.3. In this act, informed consent means a consent issued on the basis of sufficient information from the health care staff, see Article 7.

6.4. An informed consent under this chapter may be written, oral or, due to the circumstances, tacit.

6.5. The Minister for Health issues further regulations on the format and substance of the consent.

Article 7

The patient has the right to obtain information regarding his or her state of health and concerning the treatment options, including information about risk of complications and side-effects.

7.2. The patient has the right to decline information under the first paragraph of this article.

7.3. [...]."[3]

1.
The Patients' Rights Act of 1998, PRA.

2.
PRA, Article 1.

3.
This part of the provision deals with the procedures and the substantive requirements regarding information and consent. In addition, it contains an authorisation to the Minister of Health to issue further regulations.

In principle, treatment of a mentally competent person over 15 years of age may be initiated only if the concerned party consents upon receipt of information regarding his or her state of health, and concerning the treatment options and the potential risk of complications and side-effects.[1]

Information should be given to the patient only if it is possible and only to the extent that, presumably, it does not violate the patient's interests. The patient may revoke the consent at any time and waive treatment.[2]

The patient may exercise the right to self-determination in such a manner that only some types of treatment are refuted, for example infusion of blood or blood products. There is a strong presumption that a patient who does not want life-prolonging treatment will be interested in palliative measures.

To emphasise that the principle concerning patients' right to self-determination applies to mentally competent, terminally ill persons, a specific and explicit provision was added to the Patients' Rights Act of 1998:

> "A terminally ill patient may waive treatment which might only defer the moment of death."[3].

Other provisions state that deliberate wishes to go on hunger strike as well as wishes not to receive blood should also be respected.[4]

Advance statements in a current situation of illness

In connection with a current situation of illness where it can be foreseen as a likely possibility that treatment will be futile, the patient may exercise the right to self-determination by stating his or her will in advance. Such an advance statement should be respected, even if the patient later becomes incompetent, for example due to unconsciousness.[5]

A patient's wishes regarding discontinuation of treatment

The rules concerning aid in dying cover "initiating" as well as "continuing" life-prolonging treatment. However, the law presupposes that a patient has no right to request a discontinuation of treatment when death is not imminent, if compliance

1.
More detailed regulations and guidelines have been stated in governmental Order No. 665/1998 issued by the National Board of Health and Guidelines No. 482/1998 regarding informed consent.

2.
PRA, Article 6, paragraph 2.

3.
PRA, Article 16, paragraph 1.

4.
PRA, Articles 14 and 15.

5.
See administrative Regulation No. 157/1998, Article 8, paragraph 2.

with the patient's wishes would lead to the concerned party's immediate death.

The physician's authority to abstain from initiating treatment

Under certain circumstances, it may be justifiable to abstain from initiating life-prolonging treatment due to an objective allocation of the available resources in relation to this specific patient's and other patients' treatment options and prospects.

The physician's authority regarding discontinuation of treatment

In principle, a physician does not have the legal authority to discontinue treatment of a mentally competent, terminally ill patient, even though it is probable that the patient's life will rapidly expire. Normally, the patient's consent to such dispositions will be required. However, continuation of treatment which is considered "directly futile" or which is in violation of the profession's ethical code might be refused, for example if required due to an objective estimate of the optimal resource allocation. As already stated, more substantial reasons are required to discontinue treatment than to abstain from initiating it.

Mentally incompetent patients

Urgent treatment

In principle, consent from a permanently incompetent patient's closest relative is required in order to initiate or continue treatment.[1] However, if the need for treatment is acute, a health care professional is normally under an obligation to perform vital or otherwise urgent treatment immediately and without seeking the consent of a proxy. This rule applies whether or not the patient permanently or only temporarily lacks the ability to give an informed consent. A number of statutory provisions deal with this issue. The Penal Code covers such obligations in some general provisions in Articles 250 and 253.

> "Anyone who reduces some other person to a helpless condition or abandons in such a condition any person standing under his custody is to be punished [...]"[2]

1.
This principle was formalised and codified in 1998 with the enactment of PRA, Article 9.

2.
Penal Code, Article 250.

"By [...] is anyone punished who, despite that it was possible without substantial risk or sacrifice for himself or others, omits

1. in accordance with his ability, to help somebody whose life is in apparent danger, or

2. to take such measures, which under the circumstances are required for the rescue of somebody apparently lifeless, or which are prescribed for the care of persons who are subject to shipwreck or another similar accident."[1]

The Physicians' Act, Article 7, contains a specific regulation on first aid:

"Any physician is under an obligation to perform on request the first necessary medical aid when expedient medical assistance according to the available information must be regarded as acutely necessary, as in the case of poisoning, major haemorrhages, attacks of suffocation [...]."

The Patients' Rights Act includes a statute regarding cases, where there is an urgent need of treatment:

"If a patient who, temporarily or permanently, lacks the ability to give informed consent or is under the age of 15 happens to be in a situation where immediate treatment is needed for the survival of the patient or to improve the patient's chance of survival in the longer term, or for a significantly better result of the treatment, a health care professional may initiate or continue treatment without the consent of the patient or parental guardian, close relative or legally appointed guardian."[2]

Due to a provision introduced in the Patients' Right Act, patients who are permanently incapable of giving informed consent have been guaranteed an influence on treatment according to the degree to which they comprehend the situation, whether or not a legal proxy's consent is given.

"A patient who himself cannot give informed consent shall be informed and included in deliberations regarding the treatment to the degree that the patient understands the treatment situation, unless this might harm the patient. The patient's manifestations shall be taken into account to the degree that they are current and relevant."[3]

1.
Penal Code, Article 253.

2.
PRA, Article 10.

3.
PRA, Article 11.

Situations with a right or duty to abstain from life-prolonging treatment

Health care professionals have been vested with a rather wide authority to make decisions to renounce futile life-prolonging treatment in certain instances where mentally incompetent and terminally ill patients are no longer able to exercise their right to self-determination in a legally relevant manner. Primarily, this right to omit initiation or continuation of treatment has a practical impact when such measures can only defer the moment of death briefly. The Patients' Rights Act includes an explicit provision in this regard.

> "If an irreversibly dying patient is no longer able to exercise his right to self-determination, a health care professional may abstain from initiating or continuing life-prolonging treatment [...]."[1]

In another statute, the PRA defines life-prolonging treatment:

> "By life-prolonging treatment is meant treatment where there is no prospect of cure, improvement or palliation, but which only prolongs life."[2]

In a legal sense, a patient is considered terminally ill when it is highly probable that death will occur within days or weeks despite application of available treatment options. The PRA presupposes that it is a purely medical judgment to assess whether the patient is terminally ill.

The physician is also entitled to abstain from life-prolonging treatment in certain instances where the patient is not terminally ill, but where it can be assumed with great certainty that the patient will be permanently detached from every kind of genuine human contact, for example because respiratory failure after a heart attack has caused grave, irreversible brain damage. Patients in a comatose, pseudo-comatose, or a persistent vegetative state might also be mentioned in this context. The law concerning such cases is somewhat unclear, and fundamental ethical and legal issues regarding discontinuation of treatment for such patients have not been the focus of debate in Denmark.

1.
PRA, Article 16, paragraph 2.

2.
PRA, Article 17, paragraph 3.

Treatment in the case of persons who attempted to commit suicide

Traditionally, Danish courts have stipulated an extensive duty to assist an unconscious person who has attempted suicide in getting appropriate life saving treatment, even in cases where the would-be suicide has announced a wish to die and a request that others respect that wish.

If a mentally competent person is still conscious after a suicide attempt and still rejects help, such a request should be respected. In relation to such persons, no obligation or right to instigate involuntary measures to thwart suicide preparations exists. However, a suicide attempt marked by apparent dramatic circumstances probably gives others the right to intervene, for example to stop a haemorrhage. Clinically, there is a clear tendency to treat suicidal patients as mentally incompetent, which often implies transfer to a psychiatric ward.

Living wills

In connection with the codification in 1992 of the general principle regarding informed consent, explicit rules concerning living wills were enacted. A legally valid living will is a particular type of statement by which a mentally competent person of more than 18 years of age (the testator) requests to be free from futile life-prolonging treatment should the concerned party end up in a condition where the right to self-determination cannot be exercised by other means. The legal definition of a living will is now phrased like this:

> "Anyone [...][1] may establish a living will. In the living will, the concerned party may express wishes regarding treatment if he or she should later come to be in a condition where he or she can no longer exercise his or her right to self-determination[2]

A living will may include statements to the effect that:

1. the testator does not want life-prolonging treatment in a situation where he or she is irreversibly dying, and

2. the testator does not want life-prolonging treatment in the case that illness, progressed decrepitude, accident, heart failure or the like has caused such grave invalidity that the testator will be permanently unable to take care of himself or herself, physically and mentally. The Minister for Health issues further

1.
In principle, a living will may be established by anybody who is over the age of 18 and not under legal guardianship regarding personal issues, for example health conditions, see Article 13 of the PRA which does not mention Article 9 concerning permanently incompetent patients and therefore cannot be applied in relation to living wills

2.
PRA, Article 17.

regulations regarding the establishment, format, filing, revocation, etc., of living wills.[...]"[1]

With respect to situations covered by point 1 of Article 17, paragraph 2, of the PRA, it is determined in Article 17, paragraph 5, that the testator's request to omit treatment, if the patient becomes terminally ill, is binding on health care professionals. The law requires that only the assessment of the patient's medical condition be taken into consideration. Other factors, for example the physician's personal preferences, research interests or economic motives, should not be taken into account.

With respect to situations covered by point 2 of Article 17, paragraph 2, of the PRA, it is determined in paragraph 5, part 2, that the testator's request is not binding on but only guidance for health care professionals, and should be taken into consideration as such. These instances include conditions in relation to severe brain damage, among these dementia and aphasia, and also serious lung diseases and spinal disorders.[2]

In these instances, treatment is not futile, but prolongation of the patient's life implies existence in a severely impaired condition. The law presupposes that the request in such a living will may only be overruled for very substantial reasons. The physician might take a number of factors into consideration, for example the nature and progression of the illness, the treatment options, the patient's age and life situation, the relatives' opinions, etc. The physician's discretionary power in this respect is rather wide and vague.

Procedures concerning living wills

The Ministry of Health has set up a national Living Will Data Bank. The establishment of a living will under the Patients' Rights Act should be made in writing and filed with the data bank. A standard formula issued by the National Board of Health presents the two above-mentioned scenarios in brief and you can tick off one of them or both if you wish to waive life-prolonging treatment in the situations described.[3] The official formula is included

1.
PRA, Article 17, paragraph 2.

2.
Such examples are listed and described in administrative guidelines issued by the National Board of Health.

3.
A comprehensive set of administrative regulations has been issued by the Ministry of Health and the National Board of Health. The Ministry of Health has issued governmental Order No. 663/1998 on living wills. Under this order, the National Board of Health has issued administrative Regulation No. 482/1998 and administrative Guidelines No. 158/1998 regarding physicians' duties concerning living wills, etc.

in a small leaflet displayed in public places such as libraries and pharmacies. The brochure gives information on the rules and also contains a page with the living will formula, which can be filed with the Living Will Data Bank. Subsequently, the testator will receive a receipt. Three weeks later, the living will comes into effect. A modest fee of 50 DKR is required.

If a patient's condition is covered by the descriptions in the law and the physician responsible is considering life-prolonging treatment, he or she is under an obligation to check with the Living Will Data Bank whether or not the patient has filed a living will:

> "If a health care professional, in instances where patients are not themselves able to exercise their right to self-determination, is considering initiating life-prolonging treatment of an irreversibly dying patient, or is considering initiating life-prolonging treatment in a situation covered by point 2 of paragraph 2, the health care professional shall contact the Living Will Data Bank [...] to check if a living will has been filed."[1]

A testator may always revoke the living will by issuing a written and clear notification to the Living Will Data Bank. In connection with current illness, the living will may informally be revoked by a plain statement, for example to the responsible physician or another health care professional.

As at 17 December 2002, a total of 74 033 persons had filed living wills with the Living Will Data Bank. This is almost three times the number of members of the former National Association "My Living Will". Every day, between 10 and 20 living wills are filed. Some 80% of the testators are over 45 years old, so a substantial number of older people file a living will. Twice as many women as men establish a living will. During recent years, these statistics have been rather stable.

The physician's obligation to contact the Living Will Data Bank comes into effect only if initiation of life-prolonging treatment is being considered. On a weekly basis, only a couple of contacts are made by physicians to the data bank.

The enactment in 1992 of legal provisions on informed consent and living wills implied a certain clarification of the law, but neither caused drastic changes in the substantive rules nor in the medical profession's attitudes or clinical practices as these had gradually developed.

Relieving terminally ill patients from suffering ("the double effect")

Alleviating remedies may be administered if a patient is terminally ill, even though such measures might accelerate the moment of death. An explicit provision to that effect was enacted in 1992 and is now to be read in the Patients' Rights Act:

> "An irreversibly dying patient may receive analgesic or similar remedies, which are necessary to alleviate the patient's plight, even if this might cause an acceleration of the moment of death."[1]

If the patient is mentally competent, the justification of the mentioned practices requires that the rules concerning informed consent are followed. If the patient is unconscious or otherwise incompetent, the physician responsible is vested with discretionary powers to make the necessary decisions.

In medical circles, a flawed notion has prevailed which suggests that even competent and carefully administered pain treatment involving opioids always involves a significant risk that the moment of death might be accelerated due to the patient's severe respiratory depression. Recently, however, specialists have stressed that such a risk is minimal if the treatment is carried out cautiously. The risk is manifest only in rare cases where a patient quickly develops a condition involving severe pain which requires high doses of opioids. It is only in such extraordinary situations that the rules regarding the double effect are of direct clinical relevance. In the literature as well as in clinical practice there has been a clear tendency to assign a much broader field of application to these rules than is warranted by clinical experience.

In principle, legal justification of the double effect requires that the administration of alleviating remedies is not performed

1.
PRA, Article 16, paragraph 3.

with the aim of causing death. Likewise, it would clearly be illegal to initiate an automatic and continuous increase in opioid medication. From a legal perspective, such a practice involves homicide if the primary aim of the action is to terminate the patient's life. However, it might be difficult to prove intent *(mens rea)* on the part of the health care professional. A physician should always conduct a concrete, careful and conscious assessment of the patient's condition and the prognosis for improvement as well as the treatment options. Failure to meet this requirement might involve responsibility under the Physicians' Act regarding "more serious or repeat neglect in fulfilment of the mission".[1] Less aggravating violations might lead to criticism by the National Medical Complaints Tribunal.

The National Board of Health has issued a set of guidelines on the administration of a morphine drip.[2] The guidelines stress that a morphine drip is a last resort *(ultimum refugium)*, only to be applied if other infusion methods cannot be utilised. Furthermore, it is enjoined that the decision to initiate a morphine drip should be recorded in the patient's file, specifying treatment indication and dosage calculation. Continuous recording of the patient's condition should be made in the file, and any change in the dosage should be explained. The guidelines also detail the calculation of dosage and stress that the dosage may not be increased automatically, but only according to the patient's individual needs.

The Danish Medical Association harshly criticised the guidelines and claimed that they were vitiated by factual misinformation and fundamentally in conflict with the intentions behind positive legal statutes. Administration of a morphine drip under the guidelines might be interpreted as the launching of legalised active euthanasia.

The guidelines do not take into account that palliative efforts always require an individual assessment of the patient's condition. Instead, they give precise instructions regarding dosages without scientific support. The Chairperson of the Medical Association even characterised the guidelines as a "cookbook" for active euthanasia. The guidelines focus in a unbalanced way on a single facet of palliative care which may lead to more

1.
See the Physicians' Act, Article 18.

2.
Guidelines of 6 December 1995 regarding continuous intravenous opioid infusion to terminally ill patients, issued by the National Board of Health.

frequent administration of intravenous infusion of opioids as an accepted treatment measure, so long as the suggested dosage calculation is followed. In addition, it makes no sense that the guidelines distinguish between a "terminal phase" and a "completely terminal phase". The Medical Association requested that the guidelines be withdrawn or at least amended. This, unfortunately, has not happened.

Despite the obvious flaws in the guidelines, their promulgation may to some extent have counteracted tendencies towards too excessive practices in the administration of morphine infusion.

On active euthanasia: killing on request/assisted suicide

No influential Danish politician or political party or organisation has campaigned in favour of legalisation of active euthanasia. No bill has been proposed in parliament regarding decriminalisation of assisted suicide or killing on request. In many connections, medical associations and nurses' organisations have dissociated themselves from such ideas. Likewise, nearly all seventeen members of the Danish Council of Ethics have recommended maintaining the present prohibitions and aim systematically at developing palliative measures.[1]

According to Danish law, consent from the concerned party can never justify killing. In principle, mercy killing is a criminal offence, too, under the Penal Code's provision concerning homicide.[2] This is the law even if the perpetrator is a physician or a close relative.

However, the Penal Code includes two mitigating provisions regarding active aid in dying, namely Article 239 on killing on request, and Article 240 on assisting in suicide. Sentencing under these articles is relatively lenient:

> "Anyone who kills another at that person's definite request is punished by up to three years' imprisonment or no less than sixty days' lenient imprisonment.[3]

> Anyone who gives aid to a person who takes his own life is punished by a fine or lenient imprisonment. If the act is performed due to selfish motives, the punishment is up to three years' imprisonment."[4]

1.
The Danish Council of Ethics, *Medical aid in dying? A Report*, Copenhagen, 1996.

2.
The Danish Penal Code, Article 237.

3.
Penal Code, Article 239.

4.
Penal Code, Article 240.

Even if a perpetrator were to be convicted of homicide, his or her altruistic motives (for example, if the act was one of mercy) might be taken into consideration as a mitigating factor in sentencing. Likewise, it might have an impact on sentencing if the offender is perceived to have suffered enough, or to have acted under irresistible stress, for example out of compassion for the suffering of the victim.

In a case initiated in 1997 (Plejebo-sagen), which received publicity worldwide, charges were dropped against a nurse employed at a home for elderly people. Initially, she was accused of killing twenty-two seriously ill clients by administering allegedly excessive dosages of opioids. Since it was not possible to assess the specific causes of death, the district attorney later announced that, due to lack of sufficient evidence, there would be no indictment filed. Subsequently, the woman received substantial financial compensation for two months' confinement in pre-trial custody. Afterwards, the nurse gained a certain media status as an alleged victim of a miscarriage of justice and media exploitation.

In the same case, a physician in general practice was indicted for five incidents of manslaughter and violation of provisions in the Physicians' Act regarding medical malpractice. The physician had neglected to conduct the necessary medical investigations, she was responsible for a number of wrong prescriptions, her patients' records were incomplete and death certificates issued by her were nearly all deficient. Some of her prescriptions had been made by telephone and fax without personal assessment of the individual patient's condition. She was acquitted of manslaughter and fined for only two out of five counts of malpractice, while the other counts were by then legally prescribed. The case illustrates the delicate distinctions implied in relation to legal accountability in cases regarding euthanasia and other types of medical aid in dying.

In the current Danish health service system, seriously ill patients are, in the main, guaranteed the right to die a dignified death. Patients and physicians have been given rights to waive futile treatment and to employ the necessary alleviating remedies, even though the patient's life might thereby be somewhat shortened. Patients may even waive treatment that is not futile, but which on the contrary — with its high probability of success and little attendant stress – is necessary for survival.

In the Patients' Rights Act, the legislature has stated that a mentally competent person of more than 15 years of age may waive life-prolonging measures in a treatment situation as well as in advance by establishing a living will. The patient's right to self-determination should almost always be respected, but the living will becomes binding on the physician only if the patient becomes terminally ill.

In instances where a terminally ill and now mentally incompetent patient has not waived life-prolonging treatment in an advance statement, the physician is given relatively wide discretion in decisions that might imply a certain shortening of the patient's life. The physician may decide against treatment which would only prolong the dying process. Furthermore, the physician may administer alleviating remedies which can accelerate the moment of death.

In essence, the patient's own views and wishes are to be given decisive weight. However, if the patient lacks the mental competence to exercise the right to self-determination, overall priority is given to making the final part of the patient's life as comfortable and dignified as possible.

Under Danish law, active euthanasia is a criminal offence. Neither physicians or others may assist in suicide or kill on request. However, health service authorities, as well as prosecutorial agencies, are very reluctant to indict health care professionals on such offences. No physician has ever been convicted of active euthanasia.

Danish law has come a long way and legislators have managed to strike an ethical balance which gives self-determination the place it deserves, whilst avoiding the risks of legalising active euthanasia. In clinical practice, there is obviously a grey area, and active euthanasia is probably performed to a certain extent. However, a grey area will exist no matter where the balance is struck. The Danish Council of Ethics regards it as highly preferable and recommendable to maintain that area where it is under current Danish law, rather than to further legalise still more types of euthanasia.

Georgia – End-of-life care

by Givi Javashvili in co-operation with Guram Kiknadze

The protection of patients' rights has been a priority of the human rights movement over the last two to three decades in most European countries. Among the issues connected with the protection of patients' rights, paramount importance has been attached to the problem of terminally ill patients, their medical care and the protection of their dignity.

In spite of the fact that the ethical and legal issues related to the care of terminally ill patients have not been publicly discussed in Georgia, the problem is reflected in our country's legislation. Furthermore, there is a move towards formulating standards of care for terminally ill patients.

Brief historical review: euthanasia in the legislation of Soviet Georgia

Since 1921, when Russia annexed Georgia, the former's overall influence on the latter has been considerable. In this connection, it seems well worth mentioning an event that took place in 1922, during the era of the bolsheviks in Russia: a Criminal Code was adopted which said that homicide of a person asking to be killed should not be punished.[1] This was tantamount to legalising euthanasia. However, the above-mentioned provision was enforced for only a very short time (until 11 November 1922). The legislative bodies cast doubt on the rationale for such a provision, on the grounds that it might make it easier for certain people to commit evil acts. Consequently, as the commentators point out, the Russian Criminal Code went from one extreme (full impunity) to the other (appropriate punishment for what was seen as deliberate murder) in a short space of time.

Since then, according to Soviet criminal law, the killing on request of a sick person on compassionate grounds has been punished as if it were an ordinary deliberate murder.

In the 1970s, a number of Georgian lawyers raised the question of the need to make separate provision in criminal law

1.
Criminal Code, paragraph 143.

whereby a murder committed at the request of the victim, when the "murderer" is driven by compassion for the person who is suffering, is deemed to be murder committed with extenuating circumstances. All this was of course considered in the context of euthanasia and the patient-doctor relationship. At the time, murder committed without aggravating circumstances was punished by five to twelve years' imprisonment, which might or might not be followed by five years' exile.

Even if a judge wanted to take account of the patient's appeal to motives based on compassion for the victim, it was compulsory to sentence the guilty person (and that included doctors) to five years' imprisonment. On the other hand, a judge could completely disregard such circumstances and hand down a more severe sentence (up to twelve years' imprisonment plus exile). In the light of the above, one lawyer saw fit to make amendments to the Criminal Code that took account of the motives for killing, whereby "killing of a patient on request and out of compassion shall be punished by six months' to five years' imprisonment".

It can therefore be concluded that there was clearly a tendency in Georgian case-law to treat euthanasia differently from unadulterated murder and to consider an entreaty on the part of the patient and compassion for the patient as extenuating circumstances when cases involving the killing of a person who was suffering came to trial. This attitude is borne out by the fact that several Georgian authors frequently referred in favourable terms to the Criminal Codes of the times (the 1970s) in various countries (Switzerland, Norway, Finland, Greece), under which euthanasia was considered to be killing carried out under extenuating circumstances. It should be emphasised that, at the time, it was thought that there was no justification for demanding impunity for euthanasia. The various arguments that used to be put forward against euthanasia (for instance, the possibility that a doctor might be mistaken when diagnosing an incurable disease or that others might influence a patient's decision) included one based on the belief that the "legalisation" of euthanasia would undermine the prestige of the medical profession.

Accordingly, the attitude towards euthanasia was based on a compromise: namely, that it should be prohibited but was at the same time understandable, and that the punishment should therefore be less severe.

Contemporary Georgian legislation on human rights in respect of health care

In 1997, Georgia introduced legislation designed to protect human rights in the areas of health and biomedicine, in accordance with international standards. The main legislation on health and human rights, including problems related to the medical care of terminally ill persons, is comprised of the following laws and international treaties:

– Georgian Law on Health Care;[1]

– Georgian Law on Patients' Rights;[2]

– Georgian Law on the Transplantation of Organs of Human Origin;[3]

– Georgian Law on Medical Practice;[4]

– Council of Europe Convention on Human Rights and Biomedicine.[5]

The Law on Health Care passed in 1997 includes a separate chapter on the issues of medical care for terminally ill patients (Chapter XXIV – Critical conditions, death and euthanasia). This chapter emphasises the need to protect a terminally ill patient's dignity:[6]

"Treatment of terminally ill patients [...] shall be carried out with due respect for their dignity."

It should be stressed that Georgian legislation on health care, biomedicine and human rights addresses the above problem in terms of both rights and responsibilities. On the one hand, the legislation gives patients definite rights, which they can enforce via the courts, including the right to compensation (for example, the Law on Patients' Rights). On the other hand, the law obliges doctors to respect and protect patients' rights and provides for concrete sanctions against doctors who violate patients' rights (for example, the suspension or withdrawal of their licence). In addition, the Criminal Code provides for

1.
Law No.1139-Is, passed by the Georgian Parliament on 10 December 1997.

2.
Law No. 283-IIs, passed by the Georgian Parliament on 5 May 2000.

3.
Law No. 160-IIs, passed by the Georgian Parliament in February 2000.

4.
Law No. 904-Is, passed by the Georgian Parliament on 8 June 2001.

5.
The convention was signed by Georgia on 11 May 2000 and ratified by the Georgian Parliament on 27 September 2000; the official instrument of ratification was submitted to the Council of Europe on 22 November 2000 and the convention entered into force on 1 March 2001.

6.
Law on Health Care (1997), Chapter XXIV, paragraph 147.

specific sanctions relating to medical malpractice, which even go so far as the imprisonment of medical personnel in certain circumstances.

Georgian legislation on euthanasia and physician-assisted suicide

As mentioned, the problem of euthanasia is not new in Georgian legislation. Current legislation prohibits euthanasia. The Law on Health Care defined euthanasia as "helping a dying person to put an end to his or her life at his or her request".[1]

In 2002, several amendments were made to the law, including an amendment to the definition of euthanasia. So, currently, the Law on Health Care defines euthanasia as:

> "intentionally putting an end to the life of a patient in the final stages of an incurable disease".

The definition of euthanasia in current legislation thus implies a doctor's active participation in putting an end to the patient's life and not just the provision of help. When the above amendment was prepared, there was an attempt to provide for the concept of "physician-assisted suicide", which it was also intended to prohibit. The first draft of the amendment included a definition of physician-assisted suicide (helping a patient to put an end to his or her life at his or her request, for example by prescribing a lethal drug). Later on during the discussions of the draft amendments, however, a number of experts considered it irrelevant to introduce the above concept and prohibit it separately from euthanasia.

As for the prohibition of euthanasia, the Georgian Law on Health Care clearly specifies that all persons, and not just medical personnel, are prohibited from carrying out or participating in euthanasia. The relevant article of the law reads as follows:

> "No member of the medical profession or other person may carry out euthanasia or participate in the latter."[2]

It is worth mentioning that the Georgian Criminal Code[3] also prohibits euthanasia to all intents and purposes by providing

1.
Law on Health Care, Article 3.

2.
Ibid., Article 151.

3.
Criminal Law of Georgia, Law No. 2287 RS, passed on 22 July 1999.

for punishment in the event of such action. It does not, however, specifically use either the word "euthanasia" or the terms "medical profession" or "patient". The relevant article reads as follows:

> "Killing upon a dying person's firm request and in accordance with his or her genuine wishes in order to relieve him or her of severe physical pain shall be punished by imprisonment of up to five years."[1]

It should be noted that, in practice, the term "euthanasia" in Georgian legislation implies only active euthanasia. Passive euthanasia, which implies hastening the end of the life of a terminally ill person by withholding or withdrawing life sustaining treatment, is not currently perceived as euthanasia. As stated below, the issue is discussed in the context of a patient's right to refuse any kind of medical intervention.

Georgian legislation on the right to refuse treatment and on advance instructions

As is the case in the legislation of other European countries (as Georgia has been a member of the Council of Europe since 1999, the issue is now discussed in a European context), the basis of patients' individual rights is the principle of informed consent. Georgian law prohibits any kind of medical intervention without the patient's informed consent.

Nowadays, therefore, if a patient in Georgia has the capacity to take a decision, he or she has the right to refuse any kind of treatment, including resuscitation and life sustaining treatment (under the laws on health care and patients' rights). Moreover, Georgian law stresses that terminally ill patients also have these rights. Below is an extract from the Law on Health Care:

> "A capable patient in the terminal stages of a disease who is able to make a recognisable decision has the right to refuse resuscitation and life sustaining or palliative treatment."[2]

This right of a patient implies a clear ban on medical intervention against his or her wishes.[3]

1.
Criminal Code, Article N110 – Killing on a victim's request. The above version of the article is dated 30 June 2000. The former version of the same article (dating from 1999) provided for three years' imprisonment for the same offence. We were not able to ascertain either from the literature or from lawyers or legislators why the penalty for carrying out euthanasia was made more severe a year after the law was passed.

2.
Law on Health Care, Article 148.

3.
Law on Patients' Rights, Article 23.

Decisions about the care of a terminally ill person are often, of course, made by relatives. Moreover, there is no established practice in Georgia of issuing advance instructions regarding terminal care (although current legislation in Georgia does make it possible to issue such instructions). Under national legislation, relatives are entitled to refuse to allow treatment and care for the dying patient if their decision is designed to preserve his or her dignity. Another important precondition when relatives refuse to allow treatment is that the views and wishes of the patient[1] be taken into consideration.

In discussing the right of relatives to make decisions on behalf of a patient receiving terminal care, mention should be made of the means of protecting patients from relatives who abuse their right to make decisions on their behalf. Georgian legislation gives the doctor the right to disregard relatives' decisions when he or she considers the decision in question to be contrary to the patient's health interests. On the one hand, if there is sufficient time, given the patient's state of health, the doctor can apply to a court, asking for an impartial decision.[2] On the other hand, if the patient is not able to make a decision (for example, when the patient is unconscious, or in the case of a minor child) and is in need of immediate life saving medical treatment, the doctor is entitled to take a decision in the light of the patient's health interests.[3]

Under current legislation, advance instructions are part of the decision-making process relating to the medical care of dying patients.[4] Citizens are entitled to issue instructions in advance concerning their medical care. Under the Law on Health Care, however, such instructions must cover matters relating only to end-of-life care. Subsequently, in 2000, the Law on Patients' Rights slightly broadened the scope of advance instructions, and they may now express the wish not to be subjected to resuscitation and life saving treatment when the disease is about to cause severe disability.[5]

To conclude, Georgian citizens are entitled to express their wishes (consent or refusal) in advance with regard to the provision of resuscitation, life saving treatment or palliative care

1.
Law on Health Care, Article 148, paragraph 2.

2.
Law on Patients' Rights, Article 25, paragraph 1.

3.
Ibid., Article 25, paragraph 3.

4.
Law on Health Care, Article 11.

5.
Law on Patients' Rights, Article 24, paragraph 1.

should they become incompetent or lose their decision-making capacity. Advance instructions may, however, only concern the final stages of a terminal disease or a disease involving severe disability.

There is further provision in the legislation for acknowledging patients' wishes. Under the Law on Patients' Rights, everyone is entitled to nominate a person whom he or she would trust and to whom he or she would delegate the right to make a decision about medical treatment in the event of loss of decision-making capacity. It is analogous to the "durable power of attorney for health care" provided for in the legislation of the United States and other countries.

Opinion of professionals and the public on end-of-life care and euthanasia

As mentioned above, euthanasia is not yet the subject of intense public debate in Georgia. The issue has, however, been discussed in a small circle of professionals for a relatively long time. In 1999 the Georgian Health Law and Bioethics Society conducted a small-scale survey (opinion poll) among health care professionals (100 doctors representing various specialities) on the doctor-patient relationship. The questionnaire included several questions designed to elucidate the attitude of health care professionals towards the problems of end-of-life care, including the issue of withholding or withdrawing life sustaining treatment. The survey's findings differed considerably, but the prevailing attitude was that the dying patient should not have the right to choose. More specifically, the opinion poll revealed that only 27% of respondents would take into consideration the opinion of a dying patient who still had the capacity to make a decision and who asked for life sustaining treatment to be discontinued, while 28% of doctors would deliberately continue treatment regardless of the patient's opinion and the others would ask family members to make the decision. Obviously, some 70% of the respondents were not in favour of the existing legislation, which did not, and still does not, allow doctors to administer life sustaining treatment against the dying patient's wishes.

I would like to mention here an interesting article by Vakhtang Akhaladze, with a view to providing a broader picture of the views of health care professionals on end-of-life care (Akhaladze, 2001). The article sets out the opinion of an intensive care doctor, who is also a devout Orthodox Christian and theologian, on euthanasia. The author resolutely rejects the idea of legitimising euthanasia. Interestingly, the doctor predicts that a "euthanasia ideology" will take hold in Georgia as a result of harsh social conditions: when neither the government nor the public has sufficient resources to take proper care of dying patients, the state, the health service and the whole population will accept the principle of euthanasia more readily. A proportion of the public will come to believe that authorising medical killing shows greater respect for the dying patient than merely observing his or her suffering, when it cannot be alleviated.

Akhaladze considers that any attempt to legalise euthanasia is an evil crime in the eyes of society and God. Further on in the article, euthanasia is made out to be either murder (if carried out deliberately by a doctor or at the request of relatives) or suicide (if requested by the patient). The arguments put forward against legalising euthanasia include the following:

– it would devalue life and exacerbate the moral crisis;

– the public would lose their faith in health care professionals and the health system as a whole;

– it would lead to increasing crime among the medical profession.

To conclude, health care professionals strongly oppose the principle of euthanasia. Moreover, many of them find it difficult to accept the current legislation, which gives patients the right to refuse life sustaining treatment. This is sometimes considered as passive euthanasia, although it is not interpreted as such under Georgian law.

End-of-life care and the problem of resource allocation in Georgia

When considering the provision of appropriate medical care for terminally ill patients, it is necessary to address the problem of resource allocation.

As stated at the beginning of this chapter, Georgian legislation requires that end-of-life care for terminally ill patients be provided in a manner that ensures the protection of their dignity. This stipulation unquestionably implies that such patients should be provided with adequate medical care, for which purpose certain institutional and other changes are to be made: the establishment of special wards in hospitals and/or of hospices, training for health care professionals, the drafting of professional guidelines and standards for end-of-life care, and so on. Considerable financial resources need to be allocated to these tasks. In current circumstances, however, Georgia cannot afford such changes and the government has to make difficult decisions when allocating resources within the national health service. When devising state medical programmes,[1] the government has to establish priorities, such as care for newborn babies and maternity care, child immunisation, the development of primary care and preventive services, the organisation of emergency medical care for the public, and so on. At present, end-of-life care is not one of its priorities. There is, however, one exception: through local medical programmes, local authorities provide cancer patients with analgesics (painkilling drugs) free of charge. These programmes also provide for free consultations with oncologists for such patients.

On the other hand, a number of local developments designed to build up a basis for end-of-life care can be observed. Two such examples are a first small hospice set up in one of the nunneries by a small group of interested doctors and nuns and a unit set up in the Oncology Centre in Tbilisi by health care professionals interested in the issues of end-of-life care and palliative medicine. In 2003 these health care professionals planned to prepare and publish guidelines and standards concerning palliative and end-of-life care. All the above activities are financed with grants and donations.

1.
The health care system in Georgia is financed mainly through state medical programmes, which means that health care institutions receive funding earmarked for particular services rather than an overall budget, as used to be the case.

The issues of end-of-life care and euthanasia are not yet the focus of public debate. Georgian legislation is, however, quite explicit in connection with certain aspects of these issues. In particular, euthanasia is unequivocally prohibited and punishable in Georgia. On the other hand, terminally ill patients may refuse any type of care, including life sustaining treatment. Despite the fact that the Georgian state is not in a position to allocate enough resources to address the problem of adequate care for dying patients, a number of developments may be observed among an interested group of professionals, who are trying to establish the foundations for the development of palliative medicine and end-of-life care and to draw this problem to the attention of the public.

References

Akhaladze, V., "The axiological essence of disease", *Georgian Medical News*, Vol. 9, 2001, pp. 85-90.

Kiknadze, G., Javashvili, G. et al., "Georgian legislation on the health care system: brief chronological review, main stages", *Digest of Scientific Articles*, National Health Management Centre, Volume 1, 1998, pp. 15-20 (in Georgian, summary in English).

Kiknadze, G., Javashvili, G. et al., "Patients' rights legislation in Georgia", *Journal of Health Sciences and Public Health*, Vol. 1, No.1, 2000, pp. 17-26 (in English).

Tsereteli, T., "Euthanasia as a moral and legal problem", *Soviet Justice*, No. 6, 1976, pp. 35-45.

Hungary – An upcoming debate

by Bela Blasszauer

Clearly, euthanasia is not the main issue in a country where the whole health care system is on the verge of a catastrophic crisis, both economic and moral. However, in Hungary – as in other countries – it is a frequent focus of public attention. There is nothing strange in this, since death and dying are one of the most neglected aspects of health care in Hungary.

Under the communists, both the state and medicine itself were highly paternalistic. This old paternalism is still present, and shows no sign of bowing out. Most Hungarians die in hospitals, where the terminally ill experience mental and physical suffering up to the very last moment. Some people believe that only one in five has a good death, that is dies suddenly with little pain or anguish. However, not everyone sees a sudden death as a good death, since it leaves no time to settle one's affairs, forgive and be forgiven, say goodbye, and so on.

The debate on euthanasia began in the 1970s, has continued ever since and is even livelier today, now that political and moral pluralism is becoming the norm. It was something of a novelty in the 1970s and 1980s, at the time of "goulash communism", when most people felt that bribery was more or less the only ethical problem that needed airing. Not everyone welcomed the new debate, however. Indeed, some doctors thought – and still think – that bribery is enough of a problem, without giving the public something else to get worked up about. They believe that outside (lay) intrusions in the sacred realms of medicine can only cause trouble and should be avoided.

The main participants in the debate are lawyers, doctors, priests, lay people, the media and politicians. After the collapse of the communist system in 1989, this dispute, too, became vastly more colourful and exciting. As in the case of every other issue, some of the more extreme views also turned up in the media and professional journals. Even the meaning of the term "euthanasia" became controversial. There are still people who rely on definitions like the rather misleading one given, as long ago as 1924, in the highly respected *Revai Encyclopaedia*:

> "Euthanasia (Greek) meaning: reducing the pain of dying. The term denotes the doctor's efforts to relieve pain and suffering once death becomes inevitable. This can be done by administering painkillers and tranquillisers, concealing the fact that death is approaching, etc. Doctors must do nothing to hasten the process of dying, even when patients are desperate to go" (Revai, 2001).

The opponents of euthanasia claim that patients' trust will be seriously shaken if euthanasia is legalised. They will be afraid of going to hospitals where doctors act as executioners and kill off their patients. Andras Veer, former head of the National Psychiatric Institute, sees a danger that lawyers may turn doctors into executioners. He writes:

> "As far as I know, people choose to become executioners, and not everyone fancies that profession [...]. I believe that many young people will turn their backs on medicine if the law permits active euthanasia" (Veer, 1995).

Another, similar argument goes like this:

> "A doctor's prime concern must always be healing, and not the thought – 'Now, I'm going to have to kill my patient'" (Geizler, 1993).

Calling doctors executioners is plainly emotive, although everyone knows that no doctor is ever forced to practise euthanasia, any more than he is forced to carry out abortions. It is also true, however, that patients dying in unbearable pain and psychological distress cannot turn to their local car mechanic, locksmith or plumber for help – they can turn only to their doctor. The medical profession is itself divided on euthanasia. The highly conservative Hungarian Medical Association condemns it roundly and denies that it exists. TV programmes often tackle the issue, but actually do little to enlighten the public – firstly, because time is too short to discuss it properly; and, secondly, because the studio guests are usually leading medical practitioners, and the "debate" soon becomes very one-sided. An eminent heart surgeon, for example, surprised even his colleagues by saying, on one of these programmes, that patients must be told just how long they have to live. Another doctor said that euthanasia should be allowed only in rich countries, where everything was available. As a rule, there is no one on hand in the studio to question statements like this: to ask, for example, how a doctor knows exactly how long his patient will live, or what truthtelling means in clinical practice – does it mean delivering the message in straight, dispassionate, brisk (and some might say, brutal) fashion, or conveying it in humane and compassionate terms. Similarly, if euthanasia should be legalised only in rich countries, what are the poor ones – where it is also widely, but covertly practised – to do? Wait till they get rich too?

As in all other countries, some people equate euthanasia with genocide, as practised by the nazis and others, and claim that legalising it would have unforeseeable consequences. Arpad Gogl, former President of the Hungarian Medical Association and later Minister for Health, spoke for others when he declared:

> "We take an oath to preserve life, not destroy it [...]. It is an interesting question whether a lay patient, possessing little information, has the right to take a decision on ending his or her life" (Gogl, 1995).

Dr Gogl was right when he said that patients had limited information. Although doctors were legally obliged to keep their patients informed – at least following the amendment of the 1972 Health Act in 1990 – it was until recently fairly common for patients not even to know what operation had been performed on them and why. Nowadays, with informed consent a definite requirement under the "new" Health Act of 1997, most patients know far more than any of their predecessors about their illness and the proposed treatment. None the less, most malpractice suits turn on a failure to disclose information. Although banned by law, euthanasia exists in Hungary too. Passive euthanasia is certainly common, and active euthanasia occurs occasionally. Both are practised in almost total secrecy, although prosecutions are extremely rare. Indeed, Hungary's only euthanasia trial took place in the 1970s, when a newborn infant was allowed to die in a country town, and this came to light. The doctors concerned were given suspended jail sentences.

The extent to which euthanasia is actually practised can be gauged from scientific surveys published in professional journals, or from statements by leading medical practitioners, as shown in the following quotations.

Proofs of the existence of euthanasia (both forms) in Hungary

"Doctors always have to fight death, but they must also be able to accept defeat calmly when the battle goes against them. When that happens, they must not quit the field like cowards. Even as losers, they must still do everything they can to make the patient's last days easier" (Magyar, 1970).

"We do not operate on incurable patients with acute complications. If pain takes all the pleasure out of life, then we must not spare the morphine" (Boszormenyi, 1982).

"There was a woman with breast cancer. We [a team of ambulance doctors] had already been called to her a week before. When we were called a second time, we injected her with dolorgan [an analgesic]. She simply stopped breathing and died. She was young. What else could we have done? At least, we spared her an agonising death from respiratory failure" (Zacher, 1995).

"We meet euthanasia daily. If I turn off the respirator, that is euthanasia! Passive euthanasia is happening all the time – in all our wards. It is common practice, for example, when we do not give life-prolonging drugs. Passive euthanasia is universal" (ICU doctor, 1994).[1]

"Euthanasia happens frequently today, but without any legal backing. It is done secretly. In practice, both active and passive euthanasia is carried out without asking patients and getting their consent" (Matko and Kovacs, 1995).

"Faced with ethical decisions on stopping treatment in the case of severely handicapped newborn infants, Hungarian paediatricians had (like their Australian and Canadian colleagues) a permissive attitude to passive euthanasia, but were (like their Polish colleagues) almost unanimously against active euthanasia" (Schultz, 1993). (In fact, 84% of

1.
See ICU doctor: "The right to die", a two-part TV documentary made by the Balazs Bela Studio (1994) and shown several times on state and commercial TV.

> the paediatricians in Dr Schultz's survey admitted having
> been involved in decisions to withdraw treatment from
> severely handicapped infants.)

The first nationwide debate on euthanasia was triggered by the
Andrea case in 1993. Andrea, an 11-year-old patient with an
autoimmune disease, had been in and out of hospital repeatedly. She had suffered greatly, was in unbearable pain, and kept
begging her mother to put her out of her misery. Her mother,
a devout Catholic with no medical training, at last complied
and drowned her in the bath at home – out of compassion. She
was given a two-year jail sentence, but was later pardoned by
the president.

Another case was that of the "Black Angel" – a 24-year-old
nurse, who killed at least a dozen patients in a Budapest hospital.
She judged them "incurable" and set out, unasked and without
their consent, to relieve their pain and suffering forever. She
was recently sentenced to nine years in prison, and will never
again be allowed to work as a nurse. The killings were labelled
"euthanasia" by some of the media, which kept the story in the
headlines for weeks. Many hundreds of letters, mainly from
students, appeared on the Internet. The great majority of them
saw euthanasia as something based on the expressed wish of a
clear-headed adult with a terminal disease. Most accepted it as
part of the individual's right to self-determination. The following is taken from just one of those letters:

> "The present state of our hospitals (too few nurses, almost no
> hospices, low wages in health care and the bribery this causes,
> various defects in the health care system) does not suggest that
> terminally ill, bedridden patients are likely to be cared for
> humanely in the last days of their lives. Be this as it may, every-
> one has the right to preserve his or her human dignity – and is
> entitled to pain relief for that purpose" (SDF,14 May 2002).

As for extreme opinions, the following view – expressed by a
doctor – may be worth noting:

> "Imagine how unkind it would be to practise euthanasia on
> scientists, artists or writers who developed symptoms of
> dementia in old age, or on very old people with long, produc-
> tive lives behind them."

Experiments on terminally ill patients

Of course, with patients who are terminally ill, certain risks are sometimes taken – even risks which themselves endanger life. We know of experiments conducted on terminally ill persons which have had nothing to do with their actual illness. Some of these experiments are lethal in themselves, and cannot be conducted on people in good health. In the case of these terminal patients, the disease will kill them before the experiment does, and so the latter has no life shortening effect – although we cannot say this with total certainty. Research on the metabolism, involving the use of radioactive isotopes and digitalis on terminally ill patients, is one example. Because of its long half-life, the C-14 isotope can cause death eventually, when it permeates the tissues and bone marrow. We consider such experiments ethically permissible. They do not, it is true, help that patient to recover, but they contribute to scientific progress – and so prolong or save the lives of other patients (Gujas, 1995).

The Medical Association's main argument is that the doctor's duty to heal is irreconcilable with killing patients, while the Catholic Church (the country's largest) insists on the sanctity of life. The patient's right to self-determination is questioned on the grounds that sick people are incapable of taking rational decisions, and/or that lay people can neither understand nor act upon the information given to them by doctors. The obvious conclusion is doctors ought to take all the vital decisions for their patients. As for the individual doctor's conscience, it seems a little strange that "conscience" is mentioned more frequently in Hungary than in any other country in the world. The usual implication is that neither laws nor ethical rules should ever come before the doctor's own conscience, which is the surest guide to right conduct.

Terminal palliative medicine

In 1993, the Hungarian Medical Association issued a statement, which has since been incorporated into its ethical code. Essentially, this statement equates euthanasia with intentional killing of the patient, and accordingly rejects it in all its forms.

Instead, it introduces the concept of "terminal palliative medicine" – a special branch of medicine, which sets out to alleviate the physical and mental sufferings of terminal patients. The statement emphasises that doctors have the right, after due deliberation, to select any treatment they consider helpful, and to dispense with any other they judge to be futile. Either way, they cannot break the law, since their actions are based on decisions which they alone have authority to take.[1] Painstaking avoidance of the word "euthanasia" is not, of course, just a Hungarian speciality. Like other countries, Hungary has plenty of euphemisms – for example, "comfort therapy", "limited therapeutic efforts" and "reduced treatment protocol" – to cover what is, in effect, euthanasia.

The Medical Association fails to answer a number of vital questions. Why, for example, if treatment is stopped, or never even started, is this always terminal palliative medicine and never (passive) euthanasia? Palliative medicine does exist in many countries, but is merely at an embryonic stage in Hungary. So far, the State Health Insurance Fund has been (at the very least) reluctant to pay, not just for high-level pain relief, but also for spiritual, emotional, social and other kinds of support for terminally ill patients.

The medical establishment claim that all their decisions are dictated by "medical" indications. An intensive care therapist writes, for example, that "intensive therapy and resuscitation are integral parts of medicine, and as such a matter of indications" (Dezso, 1976).

At the time the statement was issued, the old Health Act of 1972, which stated that doctors must spare no pains in treating even those patients they considered incurable, was still in force. This provision actually gave doctors an almost completely free hand. After the political changeover, when the right to self-determination and human dignity was affirmed by the state, two lawyers, Albert Takacs and Ildiko Kmetty, asked the Constitutional Court, in the early 1990s, to interpret these rights as meaning that patients should decide whether or not they wanted their lives prolonged. Many years have passed since then, but the Constitutional Court has only recently

1.
See the Hungarian Medical Association's "Statement on euthanasia", *Yearbook of the Hungarian Medical Association*, 1994, pp. 33-35.

begun to consider the biggest issue it has faced so far – euthanasia. Its decision is expected in the near future.

Its dilemma is that of permitting something which is wide open to abuse, especially in a country where corruption is not – and effective control is – uncommon. In Hungary, as in many other countries, withholding treatment raises a whole series of issues: self-determination, euthanasia, professional integrity and the "doctor's conscience". Although the new Health Act (1997) does not recognise a right to euthanasia, it does allow terminally ill patients (that is, patients whom doctors expect to die "soon") to refuse life sustaining treatment. Various procedures must be gone through first (for example, a three-member ethics committee, comprising the patient's own doctor, another relevant specialist and a psychiatrist, must agree, and the patient must give his or her formal consent before two witnesses). The ethics committee must make sure that the patient is really terminal, is able to understand the consequences of his or her decision and can communicate that decision clearly. If all these conditions are satisfied, it must still try to dissuade him or her from going through with it. If it fails, the consequences of refusing treatment must again be explained to the patient. A three-day waiting period follows (during which time full life saving treatment is provided), and the patient must then be asked again, in the presence of two witnesses, whether he or she still wishes treatment to stop. If the answer is affirmative, none of the treatment planned is initiated.

The act also allows individuals to sign advance directives, refusing life-prolonging treatment. Before these can take effect, however, numerous stringent conditions must be satisfied (the person concerned must be examined by a psychiatrist when the instructions are drawn up, a lawyer must be involved, the family doctor must be notified, etc.). Such instructions can be implemented before the person concerned is actually in a terminal condition. Individuals may also appoint other persons to speak for them if they become incapable of expressing their own wishes. These "living wills" must be extended every two years, and can be revoked at any time. There is, however, a

1.
Section 47, paragraph 4.

provision in the Health Act[1] which allows a doctor to intervene at any time when a patient's life is in immediate danger – without the latter's consent. This legal shilly-shallying shows that the law can actually make it hard to communicate effectively with patients on their wishes concerning end-of-life care.

Opinion polls

It is not, perhaps, surprising that opinion polls aimed at determining attitudes to euthanasia in Hungary usually produce results very similar to those in many other countries. The most recent – a survey of 250 nurses – showed, for example, that:

- 166 (66.4%) of the respondents did not want their lives prolonged in a terminal condition, 9 (3.6%) did and 75 (30%) were unable to decide;

- 174 (69.9%) thought that patients had the right to take life-or-death decisions, 35 (14%) considered this a matter for God, 32 (12.8%) thought that doctors should decide and 9 (3.6%) left this to the state;

- 163 nurses (65.2%) thought that most patients died in inhumane conditions, 71 (28.%) thought the opposite, and there were 16 "don't-knows" (6.4%);

- When it came to defining euthanasia, 18 (7.2%) thought the term meant killing persons of limited or no value, 224 (89.6%) thought that it meant helping terminal patients to die at their own request, and 8 (3.2%) thought that it denoted a doctor's decision that it was better for a patient to die.
(Palfi and Blasszauer, 2002).

An earlier survey of ICU doctors, anaesthetists and nurses specialising in the same fields showed that 86% of doctors and 84% of nurses approved of passive euthanasia. Some 64% of doctors admitted that passive euthanasia was practised in their workplaces, and half the nurses knew of such cases. Of the 100 doctors and 100 nurses polled, it is interesting that

16 nurses, but only 4 doctors, knew about cases of active euthanasia. Some 16% of doctors, and 38% of nurses said that they would allow active euthanasia and 36% of nurses and 28% of doctors had actually been asked by patients to help them die (Fabian, 2000).

References

Boszormenyi, M., "Some practical ethical questions concerning the patient-doctor relationship", *Orvosi Hetilap*, Vol. 123, No. 25, 1982, p. 1527.

Dezso, L., "Euthanasia, or medical ethics in crisis?", *Medical Weekly*, Vol. 117, No. 22, 1976, p. 1327.

Fabian, K., "Attitudes of intensive care doctors, anaesthetists and nurses toward euthanasia", *Nover*, Vol. 13, No. 5, 2000, pp. 8-12.

Geizler, G., *Responsible decision or execution? Medical ethics in our changing world*, Szent Istvan Tarsulat, Budapest, 1993, p. 28.

Gogl, A., interview in *Magyar Orvos*, Vol. 3, November 1995, p. 8.

Gujas, M., "Medical-ethical aspects of euthanasia", *Latlelet*, Vol. 5, 1995, p. 5.

Magyar, I., "Doctors and death", *Orvosi Hetilap* (medical weekly), Vol. 111, 1970, p. 3014

Matko, I. and Kovacs, J., *The debate on euthanasia*, material prepared for the National Research Ethics Committee, 1995.

Palfi, I. and Blasszauer, B., "Attitudes toward euthanasia", unpublished survey, Faculty of Medicine and Health, Pecs University, November 2002.

Revai, *Revai Nagy Lexikona*, PC CD-Rom, digital books, 2001.

Schultz, K., "Attitudes of Hungarian paediatricians to the treatment and non-treatment of severely handicapped newborn infants – A comparative study", *Bioethics*, Vol. 7, No. 1, 1993, pp. 41-56.

Veer, A., "Euthanasia – A doctor's view", *Nepszabadsag*, 4 January 1995, p. 10.

Zacher, G., "Whose decision is it anyway?", National Conference on Patients' Rights, Budapest, 28-29 September 1995.

The Netherlands – Euthanasia as a last resort [1]

by Johannes J. M. van Delden

Although the Netherlands is an extremely flat country, it appears to have slopes that can even be skied down when it comes to euthanasia. At least, that is what many authors commenting on the Dutch experience with euthanasia want their readers to believe. Mostly those comments add up different types of end-of-life decisions. Rather than repeating our criticism that this kind of reasoning is based on unacceptable simplifications (van Delden, 1993), I would like to try to further the discussion by trying to analyse the Dutch situation. I will do so by discussing the following subjects:

- different moral frameworks for euthanasia;
- the reporting of euthanasia cases;
- the incidence of non-voluntary euthanasia.

I will use the term "euthanasia" in the Dutch way: euthanasia is the intentional ending of a patient's life at the patient's explicit request. I will treat "assisted suicide" as a variant of this: in these cases, patients take the lethal drug themselves instead of this being administered by the physician.

Moral frameworks for euthanasia

The Netherlands is often criticised for its presumed lack of palliative care. The existence of only very few hospices in the Netherlands, for example, is often interpreted as proof of neglect of palliative care. Although much of this criticism is based on misunderstanding and much effort is made to improve palliative care at present (Francke, 2003), it is certainly correct to say that the Netherlands has "some way to go in the provision of adequate palliative care". Which is, of course, also true for many other countries. But what does this mean for a moral evaluation of euthanasia?

By and large, there appear to be three ways of dealing with the issue of euthanasia (van Delden, 1999). The first is to reject it on the grounds that it is forbidden by the principle of respect

1.
Part of this chapter appeared earlier in the *Journal of Medical Ethics*.

for life. Proponents of this view often also claim that euthanasia is not necessary at all. With sincere attention to the person who requests euthanasia the "question behind the question" will surely turn out to be something other than a request to die, and with good palliative care extreme suffering need not remain unanswered. According to this viewpoint, euthanasia and palliative care are incompatible and fewer instances of euthanasia will result from better palliative care.

An alternative response to the euthanasia issue stresses the importance of compassion. From this point of view, respect for life is of paramount importance as is good palliative care. Sometimes, however, supporters of this viewpoint admit that illness and dying come with such suffering that life is reduced to pointless surviving. If all other palliative measures fail, then euthanasia may be justified. The result of this view of euthanasia is the medicalisation of the end of life, since whether or not euthanasia is justifiable becomes largely a matter of medical discretion.

These two responses appear to differ foremost in their answer to the question: "Does intractable, excruciating suffering exist?" However, even palliative care specialists will state that, unfortunately, this is true. The real difference therefore, will be whether or not one allows the principle of respect for life to be overridden by other considerations in special circumstances.

Most proposals to regulate euthanasia follow the second viewpoint. This is, by and large, also true for the new law on euthanasia in the Netherlands. This law, effective as of 1 April 2002, states in Article 2 that an act of euthanasia will not be punishable if performed by an physician who reports the case and testifies that he or she acted according to the rules of due care, namely that he or she:

a. should be convinced that the request of the patient was voluntary and well considered;

b. should be convinced that the suffering of the patient was unbearable and without prospect of relief;

c. should inform the patient about his or her situation and prospects;

d. should come to the conclusion, together with the patient, that there is no reasonable alternative solution to the situation of the patient;

e. has consulted another independent physician who has seen the patient and agrees with the evaluation of the physician on points *a* to *d*;

f. performed the euthanasia in a careful way.

Parts *b* and *d* of this article clearly create room for an independent, professional evaluation of the situation by the physician. So, even under this new law, there is no right to die in the Netherlands, nor an obligation for the physician to comply with a request of a competent patient if certain conditions are met. Therefore, my conclusion is that euthanasia is officially treated as a last resort.

The reality of the Dutch euthanasia practice, however, seems to have developed in another direction, with increasing emphasis on respect for patient autonomy. This could lead to a shift to a third approach in which euthanasia is seen as a choice. Some patients do not want to live with suffering and decline treatment, even if pain can be controlled. They want to autonomously decide about how and when to die and want their relatives to remember them as they were when they were more or less healthy. They want to step out of life before the terminal phase really starts and they want a doctor to do the lethal work.

This development is reflected in the data produced in all major studies in the Netherlands. The first nationwide study of end-of-life decisions showed that pain was hardly ever the sole reason for requesting euthanasia (van der Maas et al., 1992). In 1992 van der Wal, in an independent study, stated that 56% of requests for euthanasia were made (among other reasons) because patients thought suffering to be pointless and in 46% because they feared the decline (van der Wal et al., 1992). And the 1995 and 2001 studies show that many patients asked for euthanasia to prevent more suffering (van der Wal and van der Maas, 1996; van der Wal et al., 2003).

One may also predict (as an aside) that this emphasis on patient autonomy will lead to a change in the medical circumstances of euthanasia cases. Currently, cancer is by far the most common diagnosis (van der Maas et al., 1992; van der Wal et al., 1992). The shift towards autonomy-based decisions, however, will lead to an increase in the prevalence of situations characterised by a loss of autonomy (such as in case of dementia or after a stroke).

This emerging sense that one does have a right to die means that more palliative care does not necessarily lead to a decreasing incidence of euthanasia. From a sociological point of view, one may be tempted to interpret the shift towards autonomy-based requests for euthanasia as a side-effect of a liberal society with its emphasis on self-government, self-control and rational choice. Opponents of euthanasia will presume that they can rest their case: their prediction of a slippery slope has come true. Others will say that more emphasis on patient autonomy fits perfectly into the process of the emancipation of the patient, which has been going on since the beginning of the 1970s. They might say that it is about time to start thinking about patient decisions concerning the end of life, instead of about medical ones.

From a moral point of view, however, it should be stressed that euthanasia by a physician can never be exclusively based on respect for patient autonomy. Physicians are not in the service of patients' self-determination, they have their own job to do serving the well-being of the patient. It may be that a patient's suffering can be stopped only by ending his or her life. But in that case the physician's motive is compassion, not respect for autonomy. If this is true, and I think it is, the physician should make an independent judgment that the patient is right in considering his suffering hopeless and unbearable. Now of course protagonists of patient autonomy will argue that the question whether a person's suffering is unbearable can be answered only by that person. This view, however, is based on a misunderstanding. Granted that unbearable suffering is subjective in a certain sense, it does not follow that the person themselves is always in the best position to assess their condition in terms of even these subjective criteria. The fact that the patient's perspective is relevant (which it is, of course) does not imply that his or her assessment is final.

This has relevance for an actual development in the Dutch euthanasia debate. Part of the new law is an article to legalise living wills containing a clause in which euthanasia is requested in certain circumstances. A well-known example is the dementia clause stating that the person wishes to be "euthanised" when he or she is no longer able to recognise any close relatives or friends. But according to the second view-point I just described – which is the basic idea behind the proposal itself – it is impossible to require a physician to kill a person who, at that moment, does not want to be dead and who is not actually suffering, just because this same person (really the same person?) requested this to be done some years before. Here one can clearly see a growing tension between the prevailing view on the morality of euthanasia, which relies almost exclusively on the principle of individual self-determination, and the fact that this view has never been accepted by the law or in medical practice.

Reporting euthanasia

To accept euthanasia in an individual case is one thing, to accept it at the level of public policy is quite something else. It is often argued that proposals to legalise euthanasia can never contain absolute safeguards (Miles et al., 1997). I think this is true: there is no rule that cannot (and will not) be broken. By the way, this goes for the prohibition of drunk-driving as well. The question is whether this justifies the prohibition of euthanasia in an individual case. The Dutch tried to have it both ways by creating a public policy based on individual cases. The least one can say is that this resulted in the unsatis-factory situation of accepting and prohibiting at the same time. This created uncertainty and vagueness, both for patients and physicians, and probably contributed, to some extent, to the critical reports of the Netherlands.

Persuading the physician to bring euthanasia cases to the knowledge of the authorities is a problem of any euthanasia policy. The Dutch notification procedure helped to raise the notification rate from 18% in 1990 to 41% in 1995 and to 54% in 2001 (van der Wal and van der Maas, 1996; van der Wal et al., 2003). The government has tried to further diminish the number of unreported cases by developing a new notification procedure, in which much of the assessment is done "outside of" the legal system. Since 1 November 1998, five regional multidisciplinary assessment committees have to assess all reported cases of euthanasia. Since 2002 (under the new law), the assessment of the committees is the final evaluation (and not just an opinion) in cases judged to be delicate. Only cases in which the physician did not meet the criteria are transferred to the public prosecutor.

These committees consist of a lawyer, a physician and an ethicist. They meet approximately once every three weeks to discuss about thirty to forty cases. The outcome of these discussions can be one of three things. Mostly, the committee will conclude (perhaps after receiving further explanations from the reporting physician) that the physician has acted carefully and has met the standards. If the committee feels that the physician has not acted in a careful way, that case is handed over to the public prosecutor who will then start a legal investigation. In other cases where legal standards were met but the case was not handled sufficiently carefully from the professional point of view, the medical inspector may be alerted.

The effect of this change in procedure is not completely clear yet, but the first results can be given. In 1996, 1 700 cases were reported; and in 1997, 1 900. In the first ten months of 1998, 2 241 cases were notified to the authorities. These cases were all handled under the old system. Since the assessment committees started their work, the number of reported cases has dropped. The last two months of 1998 yielded 349 cases (resulting in 2 590 for the whole of that year). In 1999, 2 216 cases were reported; in 2000, 2 123 cases; in 2001, 2 054 cases and in 2002, only 1 882 (Regionale toetsingscommissie euthanasie, 2003). The official numbers for 2003 are not yet known, but I am certain that they will not reverse the trend shown (see Table 1). Interpreting these numbers is not without difficulty; one cannot simply deduce a percentage for the reporting of euthanasia in one year since these numbers represent only the numerator. To generate percentages one would need to know how many cases occurred in that year. The most recent nationwide study showed that in 2001 there were 3 800 cases of euthanasia and assisted suicide. Of these, 2 054, or 54%, were reported. This response is clearly less than was hoped for. Somewhat paradoxically, the new study also found that doctors in general were satisfied with the new procedure (van der Wal et al., 2003). Yet still the reporting rate lags behind

Table 1

Number of reported cases per year of euthanasia and assisted suicide in the Netherlands		
Years	Absolute numbers	% of E/AS*
1995	1 466	41
1996	1 700	
1997	1 900	
1998	2 241 + 349	
1999	2 216	
2000	2 123	
2001	2 054	54
2002	1 882	

*E/AS: Euthanasia and Assisted Suicide.

Cases of non-voluntary euthanasia

The cases of non-voluntary euthanasia were described in three reports (van der Maas et al., 1992; van der Wal and van der Maas, 1996; van der Wal et al., 2003). These reports described 1 000 cases for 1990 and 900 cases both for 1995 and 2001. These cases created a new dimension in the Dutch euthanasia debate. Since the middle of the 1980s, this debate had been focused on euthanasia and assisted suicide with the explicit request of the patient as the central feature. This in part had been a deliberate narrowing of the discussion because it was felt that consensus was closest for these cases. The Dutch even changed their definition of euthanasia to include only the cases in which there was the explicit request of the patient. Thus, a possibly justifying feature (the request) was turned into an necessary condition.

The description of non-voluntary cases has broadened the discussion again. But what does their appearance in the reports mean? Does this prove the slippery slope? Dutch commentators on euthanasia for many years talked only about cases involving a request. It is only recently that non-voluntary cases have come to light. Thus, the Dutch may have given the impression that they began with hastening the end of life on request and ended up with non-voluntary cases.

This, however, is not necessarily true. We simply do not know whether non-voluntary euthanasia occurred more or less often in the past. What we do know is that the occurrence of non-voluntary euthanasia did not increase in the Netherlands between 1991 and 2001. And also that its prevalence is much higher in other countries (Australia and Belgium) that did not slide down the slope by tolerating euthanasia year after year (Kuhse et al., 1997; Deliens et al., 2000). The Belgian numbers merit a little more attention. The percentages found for euthanasia, physician-assisted suicide and life-terminating acts without explicit request of the patient (LAWER)[1] are 1.1%, 0.1% and 3.2% respectively. The Dutch equivalents in the 2001 report are 2.5%, 0.2% and 0.7% (see Table 2). Two things are striking: there is, in sum, more active ending of life in Belgium than in the Netherlands. And also: the ratio of cases requested by the patient versus those not explicitly requested in Belgium (1:3) is the reverse of the one in the Netherlands. Perhaps, an open debate and a tolerant policy is not that bad after all.

Table 2

Incidences of Active Termination of Life in the Netherlands and Belgium (Flanders) (Percentages of Annual Mortality)				
	The Netherlands			Belgium
	1990	1995	2001	1998
Euthanasia	1.8	2.4	2.5	1.1
Assisted suicide	0.3	0.3	0.2	0.1
LAWER	0.8	0.7	0.7	3.2
Total	2.9	3.4	3.4	4.4

1.
LAWER: Life-terminating Acts Without Explicit Request of the patient.

Whilst not proving the slippery slope, the non-voluntary cases of euthanasia do represent a very serious problem. They are obviously not justified by the principle of respect for patient autonomy and therefore can only be tolerated (if at all) in extreme situations where terminating life is really the last resort and non-voluntary euthanasia becomes "mercy-killing". It is very unlikely that this was the reason behind every case described in the Dutch reports.

When reflecting on Dutch euthanasia practice and discussion one may get the impression that there are two ideologies at work. One is dominated by individual self-determination and the other focuses on compassion. Although both the official medical standpoint (Royal Dutch Medical Association, 1995) and the new law reflect the second ideology, I see a growing tension between this view and the ideas of the public, which are more autonomy-oriented. In this latter view, euthanasia becomes a right, something you can make your doctor do.

I think both systems have obvious advantages and disadvantages. The amount of liberty is clearly higher in the autonomy-oriented approach, but so is the potential for misuse of this liberty. The medicalised approach offers at least some protection against a number of these disadvantages, but at the cost of some liberty. Whatever one's standpoint, I think it is clear that the Netherlands cannot have it both ways. I think that at present there is a tendency to stretch the official medicalised approach to allow for autonomy-driven decisions. This, however, will only lead to a practice that lacks a clear picture of the moral framework within which it operates. Such a practice will be less open to any assessment procedure. After thirty years of open debate in the Netherlands that would surely be the wrong way to go.

References

Deliens, L., Mortier, F., Bilsen, J. et al., "End-of-life decisions in medical practice in Flanders, Belgium: a nationwide survey", *Lancet*, 356, 2000, pp. 1806-1811.

Francke, A. *Palliative Care for Terminally Ill Patients in the Netherlands*. The Hague, Ministry of Health, 2003.

Kuhse, H., Singer, P., Baume, P., Clark, M. and Rickard, M., "End-of-life decisions in Australian medical practice", *Medical Journal of Australia*, 166, 1997, pp. 191-196.

Miles, S., Pappas, D. and Koepp, R., "Considerations of safeguards proposed in laws and guidelines to legalize assisted suicide", in Weir, R.F. (ed.), *Physician-assisted suicide*, Bloomington, Indiana University Press, 1997.

Regionale toetsingscommissie euthanasie, *Jaarverslag 2002*, Ministerie VWS, The Hague, 2003.

Royal Dutch Medical Association, *Standpoint on euthanasia*, Utrecht, KNMG, 1995.

van Delden, J.J.M., "Slippery slopes in flat countries", *Journal of Medical Ethics*, 25, 1999, pp. 22-24.

van Delden, J.J.M., Pijnenborg, L. and van der Maas, P.J., "Dances with data", *Bioethics*, 7, 1993, pp. 323-329.

van der Maas, P.J., van Delden, J.J.M. and Pijnenborg, L., *Euthanasia and other medical decisions concerning the end of life*, Amsterdam, Elsevier, 1992 (also published as special issue of *Health Policy*).

van der Wal, G. and van der Maas, P., *Euthanasie en andere medische beslissingen rond het levenseinde*, The Hague, SDU uitgevers, 1996, p. 57.

van der Wal, G., van Eijk, J.T.M. and Spreeuwenberg, C., "Euthanasia and assisted suicide. II. Do Dutch family doctors act prudently?", *Family Practice*, 9, 1992, pp. 135-140.

van der Wal, G., van der Heide, A., Onwuteaka B. and van der Maas, PJ. *Medical decision-making at the end of life*, Utrecht, de Tijdstroom, 2003 (in Dutch).

Portugal – Euthanasia : not ethically permissible

by Daniel Serrão

This paper sets out to deal with its subject succinctly and objectively from three angles: the legal and ethical perspectives and the standpoint of public opinion.

The legal perspective

The word "euthanasia" is not used in the Portuguese Criminal Code, but this does not mean that death brought about at the victim's request will go unpunished, for the code includes the following stipulations:

"*Article 131* (homicide)
Anyone who kills another person shall be liable to imprisonment for a term of between eight and sixteen years.

Article 133 (homicide in special circumstances)
Anyone who is moved to kill another person under the influence of an understandable violent emotion, through compassion or despair, or for any other reason with a significant social or moral value that appreciably diminishes the perpetrator's culpability, shall be liable to imprisonment for a term of between one and five years.

Article 134 (homicide at the victim's request)
Anyone who kills a person of adult years and full responsibility, in response to that person's earnest, conscious, freely expressed and explicit request, shall be liable to imprisonment for a term of between six months and three years.

Article 136 (homicide through negligence)
1. Anyone who occasions the death of another person through negligence shall be liable to imprisonment for up to two years.

2. In cases of gross negligence, the term of imprisonment may be up to three years."

Under Portuguese law, conduct by members of the medical profession that brings about a patient's death, whether on the basis of a doctor's unilateral decision, at the patient's request or through negligence, is classed as homicide and is punishable by imprisonment, although the sentences may be lighter than those provided for in Article 131.

This legal doctrine is generally accepted although there is no recorded instance of a doctor being brought to trial under Article 133 or Article 134. Both criminal and civil cases have been brought under Article 136 but the negligence alleged has not been associated with an intention to practise euthanasia.

The Professional Code of Ethics of the Portuguese Medical Association, which is a quasi-legal instrument, includes, in various articles of its second chapter, relevant rules that doctors must observe. Thus:

"[...]

1. Doctors must respect human life from its inception.

2. Both abortion and euthanasia are serious breaches of professional ethics.

[...]

3. To refrain from initiating a treatment, if such is the free and conscious choice of the patient or his or her representative, does not constitute euthanasia."[1]

With regard to the prolonging of life by artificial means, the code states:

"In the case of illnesses where the prognosis is certain death within a very short time, doctors must not prolong life by artificial means when there is no hope of bringing about recovery, and may confine themselves to the provision of moral support and prescription of treatment to prevent unnecessary suffering, respecting the patient's right, as a human being, to a dignified death."[2]

It adds that:

"If the patient is in a coma with no hope of regaining consciousness, and brain function has irreversibly ceased, the decision to suspend the use of extraordinary measures to prolong life artificially must be taken on the basis of the most rigorous available scientific criteria so that there is proof of brain death.[3]

Doctors generally accept and obey these rules. There is no record of the Medical Association initiating disciplinary proceedings for failure to observe them.

1.
Medical Association Professional Code of Ethics, Chapter II, Article 47.

2.
Ibid., Article 49.

3.
Ibid., Article 50, point 1.

There is no current of opinion among Portuguese doctors in favour of active voluntary euthanasia. Within intensive care units there is much concern about the prolonging of life by artificial means and about the question of respecting the patient's wishes, whether expressed at the time or in advance.

The ethical perspective

The prevailing view is that euthanasia – considered strictly as the bringing about, by a doctor, of a patient's death at the patient's explicit request – should not be ethically permissible.

However, when the discussion is extended to include other medical approaches – suicide assisted by a doctor, nurse or close relative; the use or non-use of vital-function support; the continuance or suspension of such support; refusal by patients of particular treatments even when these may be life saving; execution or non-execution of prior written instructions (such as a will or an instruction to withhold resuscitation) – lively ethical debate ensues and opinions differ on the legitimacy of the possible decisions in each case.

The National Ethics Council for the Life Sciences has published a report on the subject,[1] and unanimously approved the opinion appended to this article.

The report "Ethical aspects of health care at the end of life" took a number of actual situations and made an ethical appraisal on each. The cases were:

1. a terminally ill patient receiving supportive medical care at home;

2. a very seriously ill patient in hospital, entering a terminal phase in which curative treatment is withdrawn and palliative care and medical support are provided;

3. an incurably ill, dying patient who asks for and receives assistance in committing suicide;

4. an incurably ill, dying patient who asks the doctor to kill him or her and who is killed;

5. an incurably ill, unconscious, dying patient whom the doctor decides to kill;

1.
I was the rapporteur.

6. a patient who has given instructions not to use certain treatments in given situations, even if death results.

Situations 1 and 2 were deemed ethically permissible; situations 3, 4 and 5 were deemed ethically impermissible; and situation 6 was regarded as debatable in ethical terms, with strong arguments for both acceptance and non-acceptance of "living wills".

Public opinion

A recent survey conducted by the Ethics Committee of the São João University Hospital, Oporto, through the Grupo de Trabalho ao Encontro da Espiritualidade do Doente (working group on meeting patients' spiritual needs), is highly informative. Doctors, nurses, care assistants and other professionals – 1 046 individuals in total – said there was a need to create appropriate facilities for the care of terminally ill and dying patients, including in ordinary hospitals (93% of replies on this question were positive). A majority of respondents felt that patients should be cared for and supported by a team comprising a doctor, a nurse, a psychologist and a spiritual assistant. As health professionals, they took the view that palliative care was an appropriate alternative to the tragic situation of the patient driven to request euthanasia.

Portuguese radio and television have been covering developments in other countries, notably the Netherlands and, more recently, Belgium. They interview doctors, lawyers, ethics specialists and ordinary people, and – where the meaning of the word "euthanasia" is not properly explained to the interviewees, due to lack of time – a range of opinions emerges.

Generally speaking, the print media take a more cautious approach, seeking the views of people with a thorough knowledge of the issues and providing quality background reporting. One example was a supplement ("Euthanasia: to live or die?") by journalist Dulce Neto, distributed with *Público*, one of the country's biggest selling daily newspapers with a very large readership in educated circles in Portugal. After an excellent introduction, with a general presentation of the euthanasia question – euthanasia being defined as "killing someone at his or her request" – and reference to the law in the Netherlands and to a range of views in that country, the supplement featured interviews with prominent figures in Portugal. These included the head of the Medical Association, who restated the position set out in the Professional Code of Ethics prohibiting doctors from practising euthanasia, a cancer specialist who agreed with the doctrine of double effect but opposed euthanasia, and a neurosurgeon and a non-medical researcher who believed the issue was an important one that had not been properly discussed in Portugal by either society or the medical profession. All condemned the prolonging of life by artificial means and accepted that patients had a right to refuse treatment. They acknowledged that many doctors lacked information on and training in proper treatment of pain and suffering. All said they had never practised euthanasia but one respondent, admitting that individual cases could be very difficult, said he had been in a situation where he ought, perhaps, to have done so. The last article in the supplement was an interview with an entirely lucid paraplegic patient (suffering from Guillain-Barré syndrome), who complained about the situation but felt, at the same time, that being able to watch his grandson growing up was a good enough reason for not wanting euthanasia.

This coverage of the issue accurately mirrors Portuguese public opinion: there is a feeling that euthanasia is acceptable in cases of intolerable suffering, but people have difficulty with the idea of making it easier or legal for doctors to "kill" patients. Dulce Neto mentions that in a recent survey in Portugal,[1] 54.1% of people regarded euthanasia as an acceptable action within certain limits, 85% accepted it unreservedly, and 35% considered it unacceptable in any circumstance.

In my personal experience,[2] where palliative care, with proper pain relief and emotional support, is put forward as an alternative to euthanasia, the percentage of opinion in favour of euthanasia falls to between 1% and 3%, representing the small group of people who believe that individual autonomy, as a value, ranks higher than life.

1.
Study entitled "Social attitudes of the Portuguese", edited by José Machado Pais, Manuel Vilaverde Cabral and Jorge Vala, of the University of Lisbon Social Sciences Institute.

2.
As a bioethics and medical ethics instructor teaching these subjects on postgraduate and higher diploma courses.

This trend in personal views about euthanasia is confirmed by the fact that in the experience of palliative care units in Portugal there is no demand for euthanasia either from terminally ill patients in their care or from the larger number of patients who receive home care under the units' supervision.[3]

It has to be recognised, none the less, that there is still a great shortage of palliative care and medical support for the terminally ill and dying in Portugal, and that both public sector health care providers and private sector non-profit-making or welfare organisations need to make a major effort to ensure that patients receive proper care as they approach death. Only when this has been accomplished will we be entitled to say that there is no ethical justification for euthanasia in Portugal and that it is not a matter of concern for society. Until then, the problem is not going to go away.

1.
I would add that the explanatory report on the Netherlands legislation, compiled for the ministries of justice and health, states: "The only sound framework within which euthanasia may be performed is that of good palliative care" (Section 2, paragraph 6).

Opinion of the Conselho Nacional de Ética para as Ciências da Vida – CNECV
(National Ethics Council for the Life Sciences)

Lisbon, 7 June 1995
Rapporteur: Daniel Serrão
Chairperson: Augusto Lopes Cardoso

Considering that the question of euthanasia in relation to various types of conduct, whether or not they occur in the course of medical activity, has been the subject of public debate both in the media and as a matter of concern to the individual about which he or she is sometimes asked;

Considering that, in a culture which denies suffering and pain and refuses to contemplate questions of death and transcendence, the matter is less likely to be mentioned or even understood;

Considering that this cultural attitude and the uncritical transmission of information in this area generate a tendency to accept the "idea" of euthanasia, as illustrated by the legislative initiative in the Netherlands and the information provided there;

Considering that, in the absence of a proper definition of euthanasia as set out in paragraphs 4 and 5 of the above report, the term is commonly applied to a range of situations;

Considering that euthanasia, like other questions about the ultimate value of life, can be analysed only in its human, axiological and ethical context;

Considering that, although euthanasia is not an acute issue in Portugal, this is the right time to address it in the interests of dispassionate, enlightened debate free of prejudices and preconceptions, the Conselho Nacional de Ética para as Ciências da Vida (CNECV) is of the opinion – based chiefly on the above report – that:

– there is no ethical, social, moral or legal case, or argument of medical ethics, for legalising the intentional termination of a patient's life (even if it is not declared or regarded as such), by anyone let alone a doctor, even if the decision to do so is taken in response to a "request" or on grounds of "compassion";

- there is thus no argument based on respect for the human person or for life that justifies acts of euthanasia;

- the withdrawal of disproportionate or ineffective treatment is ethically permissible, particularly where the treatment is causing the patient discomfort and distress; such withdrawal, even though it might shorten life, is not to be regarded as euthanasia;

- the use of medication to relieve pain is ethically acceptable even where it may have the secondary effect of shortening the patient's life, and it, too, should not be deemed to constitute euthanasia;

- acceptance of euthanasia by civil society or the law would destroy patients' confidence in their doctors and in medical teams, and could lead to unchecked "authority to kill" and to barbarity;

- refusing to recognise euthanasia as a right of each doctor (or others) and each patient (or others), none the less creates individual and social obligations that cannot be minimised or overlooked, most notably:

  - a private and public responsibility to take proper care of terminally ill patients, people with disabilities and people with all types of dependency;

  - a duty to provide sustained care for dependent people, respecting in full their integrity and dignity as human beings;

  - a duty to create and maintain conditions in which palliative care can be provided for those who need it;

  - a duty to support research on the treatment of pain, and to set up groups of specialists in this area of medicine;

  - a duty to develop a high standard of training for doctors and nurses as part of undergraduate and postgraduate courses, so that health professionals understand, and are in a position to assume purposefully, their ethical responsibilities towards their patients, particularly those who are in the terminal stages of illness and must be enabled to die with complete dignity.

References

Conselho Nacional de Ética para as Ciências da Vida (National Council of Ethics for the Life Sciences), "Opinion on ethical aspects of health care at the end of life", Presidência do Conselho de Ministros, Lisbon, 1995.

Neto, D., "Eutanásia. Viver? Morrer?" (Euthanasia: to live or to die?), *Público*, Supplement No. 308, 21 April 2002.

Grupo de Trabalho Ao Encontro da Identidade Espiritualidade do Doente (working group on meeting patients' spiritual needs), "Nós e o morrer no Hospital" (Ourselves and death in hospital), São João University Hospital, 2002.

Pina, J.A.E., *A responsabilidade dos Médicos* (The responsibility of doctors), Lidel, Edições Técnicas, Lisbon, 1994.

Switzerland – Defending assisted death

by Alberto Bondolfi

In Switzerland, as elsewhere in Europe and, more generally, in all highly industrialised countries, the question of assisted death is giving rise to a wide debate; however, certain aspects of the argument are unique to Switzerland. The purpose of this chapter is to set out the broad outlines of this debate and to assess these from a European perspective. As an ethics specialist, I will not merely provide information, I will also offer some pointers towards understanding the various issues more clearly.

What have been the salient features in this debate over the past decade?[1] In my opinion, it is difficult to isolate a single current of thought throughout the period; I believe it is more relevant to note the existence of several approaches, which intersect and overlap to establish a new and provisional balance.

Towards recognition of advance directives

Since the debate began in the 1970s, a recurrent theme in patients' testimonies has been undue persistence in therapeutic intervention. Over this period, most Swiss hospitals have opened highly specialised intensive care units, to which patients in considerable distress, but not necessarily in the terminal phase, are admitted more or less automatically. This indiscriminate transfer of patients leads to situations that are objectively unmanageable; faced with these, the medical profession has proved incapable of drawing up codes of conduct and of taking decisions that would result in an acceptable death for the patients in question, together with support for their relatives. Public opinion is outraged by the very lengthy and sometimes unjustified hospitalisation of terminal-phase patients in intensive care units.

The medical profession, for its part, aligns itself with the Swiss Academy of Medical Sciences, a highly credible and influential

1.
On this subject, see Bondolfi, A.: "Il living will nel dibattito sulla buona morte", KOS, 80, 1992, pp. 18-25; "Living will", in Dizionario di bioetica, Leone, S. and Privitera, S. (eds.), EDB-ISB, Bologna, 1994, pp. 553-556; and "Beihilfe zum Suizid: grundsätzliche Überlegungen, rechtliche Regulierung und Detailprobleme", Ethik in der Medizin, 12, 2000, pp. 262-268.

organisation (at least within the medical establishment). The academy's central ethics committee[1] expressed its opinion for the first time in 1976 in the form of guidelines, which were subsequently amended in 1981; these guidelines dealt with the subject of euthanasia (at the time, use of the term in Switzerland carried no negative connotations, since it refers to a series of measures to make death more bearable). The issue of living wills and advance directives was also addressed explicitly for the first time.

These directives are important for all doctors practising in Switzerland and for politicians because in some cases cantons may give them legal force, even indirectly. However, it may be noted that the guidelines, which are merely the result of a self-regulatory process, have no legal character.

Initially, the Swiss medical profession reacted strongly against the phenomenon of advance directives, and not only for strictly moral reasons. In reality, this rejection or reticence was linked to the fact that the expression of individual wishes seemed to limit doctors' freedom with regard to the clinical assessment of specific situations and, consequently, short-term clinical decision-making.

Doctors' reactions subsequently became more muted, and they responded to the demands that were being indirectly expressed through these directives. Thus, the Foederatio medicorum helveticorum (Federation of Swiss Doctors) produced a basic text on advance directives, compatible with the traditional view of the doctor's duties as described by Hippocrates.[2]

Other charitable or ecclesiastical organisations, such as Caritas Switzerland, have also prepared documents and texts of a similar nature. The Institute of Social Ethics of the Federation of Swiss Protestant Churches has even drawn up a provisional list of these texts, which is now distributed in Switzerland.[3]

With hindsight, it is now accepted that this reaction on the part of the medical profession and associations to giving assistance to the dying can be explained by the fact that Exit, an association which supports assisted suicide, had asked a renowned legal specialist to prepare a legal opinion on living wills and to

1.
The texts published by this body can be found at www.samw.ch

2.
See www.fmh.ch

3.
With regard to documentation: *Patientenverfügungen. Eine Materialsammlung*, ISE, Berne, 1992, (ISE-Texte 1/92); also, Die Kirchen im Kanton Bern nehmen Stellung zu Exit: Vereinigung für humanes Sterben, Arbeitsgemeinschcaft christlicher Kirchen im Kanton Bern, Berne, 1990.

envisage collaborating with it. The opinion by Dr Max Keller, Zurich, concluded that these directives should be considered as directly applicable by the physician.

Faced with this maximalist position, the Swiss Academy of Medical Sciences reacted by asking for a second opinion from two other leading legal experts, Professors Guinand and Guillod; their conclusions were not necessarily at odds with those expressed by Exit, and highlighted, above all, some legitimate demands which lay hidden behind documents of the advance directive type. The 1981 version of the academy's guidelines sought to take account of these demands, stating that:

> "If the patient has rejected all artificial prolongation of his or her life via a written declaration, the physician has a duty to establish carefully whether the conditions set out in the declaration – in so far as they correspond to the present guidelines – are met. Where there is no doubt that these conditions are met, the physician must act in accordance with the wish expressed in the said declaration, unless specific circumstances make it possible to conclude that this declaration no longer corresponds to the patient's real wishes."[1]

Through these statements, the academy finally succeeded in providing a more open interpretation of the importance of living wills, although the Swiss Minister of Justice had so far denied the legal significance of these documents.[2] Through this compromise solution, the organisation recognised in 1989 that documents of this type could indirectly reflect all sorts of feelings, including the wishes of unconscious patients, even if this form of expression could not be considered as falling within the doctor's jurisdiction.

In 1995, the guidelines were again revised, and the passage concerning living wills was reworded. In order to clarify its position, the Swiss Academy of Medical Sciences improved the coherence of these documents with regard to the physician's actions, and limited their scope by setting out the conditions in which such documents may be considered admissible. Thus, the scenario by which doctors would find themselves faced with a document providing for their active assistance in suicide or homicide is averted, since it is stated that in such cases the document would be considered void.

1.
Swiss Academy of Medical Sciences, *Medical-ethical guidelines for the medical care of dying persons and severely brain-damaged patients*, Basle, 1995, No. 3, p. 18.

2.
The text is taken from the *Neue Zürcher Zeitung*, 31 December 1987, p. 18.

"If a patient's advance directive exists, which the patient wrote at an earlier point in time when he was capable of judgment, then this is binding. However, requests requiring illegal actions on the part of the physician must of course be disregarded, and demands for the withdrawal of life supporting measures must be refused in situations in which, from experience, a return to a life of normal human communication and recovery of the will to live are to be anticipated."[1]

In recent years, discussion on advance directives has intensified, since the public has taken a close interest in the debate surrounding euthanasia and its regulation. Whatever the case, it is clear that a very wide consensus has developed in Switzerland on recognition of the primacy of the principle of autonomy when interpreting the wishes of a dying patient. Thus, a group of experts appointed by the Federal Department for Justice and Police (we will return to this group below when considering the specific issue of euthanasia legislation) reached the following conclusion in 1999:

"Wherever such termination of treatment corresponds to the patient's express wishes, the physician may not be charged with regard to this behaviour, since, in line with a legally recognised principle, any medical act requires the patient's (express or presumed) consent. If this consent is absent or has been refused, the physician's intervention must be considered as resulting from his or her own authority, and consequently as 'non-authorised'. This also applies to measures to ensure survival."[2]

The legal and political debate on assisted suicide and euthanasia

Switzerland, a country which is at the crossroads of numerous cultural and ideological influences, has in recent years seen a rekindling of interest in and a radicalisation of the debate surrounding voluntary death and assisted suicide. The purpose of this contribution is to identify the conflicting positions, together with the arguments and internal difficulties in such a debate, and finally to outline a personal position.

The beginnings of the debate

In order to understand more clearly the major issues in the Swiss debate, one must first be aware of the Swiss legislation in

1.
Swiss Academy of Medical Sciences, op. cit., No. 3.4, p. 3 (see also www.samw.ch).

2.
See the report "Assistance au décès", pp. 13-14 (see also www.ofj.admin.ch).

the area under consideration. In the section on crimes against human life, the Swiss Criminal Code punishes homicide even where it is requested by the victim (Article 114, Murder at the victim's request), although the prescribed sentence is less than that for other forms of murder.

On the other hand, Switzerland is not particularly severe with regard to suicide and third party assistance to those committing suicide. In this respect, it has shown itself more tolerant than neighbouring countries. Article 115 of the Criminal Code states, in fact, that a person who has assisted someone else in ending his or her life shall not be punished, so long as this person was not acting under the influence of a selfish motive.

These two provisions in the Criminal Code date back to the end of the 1930s and draw partially on older cantonal provisions.[1] In interpreting these criminal provisions from a historical perspective, it is important to recognise that they were not drawn up with a view to managing medical conflicts; they applied, especially where assisted suicide is concerned, to typical practices in a civilisation where people still committed suicide for reasons of honour.

None the less, recent years have seen the emergence of a debate, firstly on how to manage the terminal stages of disease and, secondly, on assistance to those committing suicide in particular circumstances. This debate has taken place either through the mass media or at a more political level, namely in the context of specialised committees and parliamentary and governmental work. I intend to focus on the latter.

As early as 1994, Victor Ruffy, a socialist member of the National Council (lower house of parliament), tabled a parliamentary motion, requiring the government to legislate; the motion was worded as follows:

> "Faced with the various degrading forms in which incurable illnesses develop, in spite of the facilities available to prolong life, more and more human beings in our society wish to have the option of playing an active role in the end of their lives, in order to die with dignity. The Federal Government is asked to submit a draft law that would lead to the addition of an Article 115 bis to the Swiss Criminal Code."

1.
For an historical survey: Pedrazzini, A., *L'omicidio del consensziente ed il suicidio nel diritto penale contemporaneo*, Tipografia Pedrazzini, Locarno, 1949.

The Federal Government, in other words the Swiss Government, did not respond to this approach (as it had done in the past) by stating that such a motion contradicted the right to life; instead, it proposed that it be changed into a parliamentary motion requesting the government to legislate ("postulat"), that is giving it a less rigid form; the National Council approved this motion in 1996. The following year, the Department of Justice and Police set up a working group to analyse the situation and draw up proposals.

In March 1999, the group submitted its report with the title "Assistance au décès" (Assistance in dying).[1] For the first time in Switzerland, this report put forward certain proposals which had been unanimously accepted by the group, and others which had only received majority support.

The most significant proposals from the first set are as follows: resources for palliative care should not only be encouraged, but fully exploited. In this context, it should be possible to guarantee the right to have care terminated. Passive euthanasia and active indirect euthanasia should not only be considered legal, but their practice should be minutely governed by legislation, even if the group declined to put forward a text specifically meeting this requirement. The cost of appropriate medical care in the final stages of human life should in no way constitute a ground or argument for legitimising euthanasia.

In addition to these points on which it reached unanimity, the group could only agree by a majority on an exception intended to form the subject of a new paragraph in Article 114 of the Criminal Code, dealing with murder committed at the victim's request:

> "Where the perpetrator ended the life of a person suffering from an incurable condition and in the terminal phase of illness, with a view to ending unbearable and irremediable suffering, the competent authority shall not bring proceedings against him or her, send him or her before the courts or impose a sentence."[2]

A minority in the group rejected this proposal, pointing out that there was no need for it where palliative measures were

1.
Can be consulted at www.ofj.admin.ch

2.
See www.ofj.admin.ch (the quotation is from p. 35 of the report).

correctly applied. They mentioned the risk of embarking on a "slippery slope" if the moral and criminal prohibitions were relaxed.

The report was discussed in the media and by political parties, thus intensifying the public debate which had already existed for several years. The Federal Government examined the report and responded in July 2000. It rejected the proposal put forward by the majority in the group but, faced with the alternative of maintaining the status quo, confirmed that it was essential to make maximum use of the possibilities offered by palliative care. With regard to passive and indirect active euthanasia, the Swiss Government took the view that these should be regulated by legislation, and did not rule out setting up a group of experts with a view to preparing such a text. As for the possibility of an exception for murder committed at the victim's request, it remained firm:

> "Even if worded in a very restrictive manner, an exception to the punishable nature of direct active euthanasia would be equivalent to a relaxation of the prohibition on homicide, and would represent the breaking of a taboo that is deeply embedded in our Christian culture."[1]

The media's reaction was divided, and the debate was continued in parliament through a parliamentary initiative, a specific legal instrument that enables a parliamentary majority to revise legislation; their decision thus becomes binding on the government.

Recent parliamentary follow-up

This was the case with regard to two parliamentary initiatives, the first submitted by Mr Franco Cavalli, oncologist, Chairperson of the Swiss Anti-Cancer League and member of the Socialist Party, and the second by Ms Vallender, a radical from Appenzell.

Mr Cavalli tried to revive the proposals made by the majority in the Department of Justice and Police working group, by introducing them in a procedure that would grant the privilege of immunity from prosecution only to doctors who had received an explicit mandate from patients to end their lives.

1.
Ibid., p. 15.

In contrast, Ms Vallender wished to ensure that the current Article 115, which provides for non-prosecution for assisted suicide in the absence of selfish grounds, was clarified to ensure that it could not be used, especially in psychiatric cases.

The National Council's parliamentary committee approved Mr Cavalli's parliamentary initiative by a majority, and rejected Ms Vallender's proposal. However, matters proceeded otherwise in the plenary assembly, where both initiatives were rejected, albeit for different reasons.

Thus, after so much discussion, Switzerland has returned, at least on a legislative level, to the previous status quo. Since parliamentary initiatives which have failed in one house may not be transmitted to the other, there will consequently be no further parliamentary debate on this issue in the near future.

Should it so wish, another body is now entitled to re-open the debate, although it acts only in an advisory capacity. This is the National Ethics Commission, a similar body to the national committees in Switzerland's neighbouring countries.[1] This organisation is responsible for advising both parliament and the government on the ethical issues raised by medical practices or biological research. Should this body express an opinion on the proposals made to date, it could relaunch the debate at parliamentary and/or governmental level.

However, this is mere speculation. In the very recent past, there have been further new developments in the practice of assisted suicide, strictly related to the more general problem of euthanasia.

The latest developments in organisations which support euthanasia

Exit, an association which has a membership of several tens of thousands in Switzerland, is not an exclusively Swiss entity, but builds on positions that have already been expressed, whether in the English-speaking countries, Germany or the Netherlands.[2] Its positions have developed in recent years and any ethical assessment should bear this in mind. If at the outset, it openly defended the legitimacy and appropriateness of a right

1.
Its positions can be consulted at www.nek-cne.ch

2.
On the discussion in these countries see, for Germany: *Alternativentwurf eines Gesetzes über Sterbehilfe*, Stuttgart-New York, 1986; and also Saueracker, L., *Die Bedeutung des Patiententestamentes in der BRD aus ethischer, medizinischer und juristischer Sicht*, Lang Verlag, Berne, 1990; for information on this historic phase in the Netherlands: Blad, J.R., "Ceci n'est pas l'euthanasie. Chronique du débat sur la mort douce aux Pays-Bas", *Déviance et Société*, 15, 1, 1990, pp. 93-121.

to "active euthanasia",[1] that is the direct ending of a patient's life by a doctor, simply on request, it has since been obliged to moderate its position to avoid the risk of conviction for incitement to crime. Subsequently, it has primarily defended the right to receive assistance with a view to committing suicide, and has put forward a series of measures to this end.[2]

Most recently, Exit and similar organisations such as Dignitas have sought to further their work in two directions: (a) by proposing assisted suicide as an option in old people's homes; and (b) by seeking to reach individuals who are not, strictly speaking, in the terminal phase but who are suffering greatly from their situation, especially psychologically.

These developments have been the subject of recent discussion, since the municipality of Zurich, which had forbidden members of Exit and similar organisations from carrying out assisted suicide in establishments for the elderly, recently granted such authorisation, albeit subject to certain very strict conditions.[3]

The city of Geneva and the Canton of Vaud are currently drawing up similar regulations authorising this practice, which is rare but none the less a reality in old people's establishments, while avoiding proselytism and taking care not to arouse concern among other residents. This debate is ongoing, and I cannot predict its future consequences.[4]

Where next?

We can already state that assisted suicide, a practice which was tolerated in criminal law, is increasingly understood by a section of public opinion as a sort of "right to commit suicide", and thus any obstacle to suicide or campaign against it is seen as the work of "over-zealous do-gooders". This observation leads me to conclude that assisted suicide and its regulation will continue to be the subject of debate in Switzerland, and that a clearer legal position than that currently set out in the Criminal Code will have to be adopted.

1.
We have placed this expression between quotation marks on account of the various misunderstandings connected with it, and we will seek to avoid its use hereafter.

2.
See *Fünf Jahre Exit*, Grenchen, 1987; in the same vein, see Burky, J.C., *La Mort dans la dignité*, Ed. Réalité socials, Lausanne, 1986; and Kehl, R., *Sterbehilfe. Ethische und juristische Grundlagen*, Zytglogge Verlag, Berne, 1989.

3.
For direct access to the file: www.stzh.ch/mm/sterbehilfe

4.
The literature is abundant, but cannot be cited *in extenso*. See, *inter alia*, Mazzocato, C., "Demande de suicide médicalement assisté ou d'euthanasie: que peut-elle cacher?", *Revue Médicale de la Suisse Romande*, 121, 2001, pp. 407-411.

As for the Swiss Academy of Medical Sciences, it claimed in its 1995 guidelines that assisted suicide is not part of a physician's activity.[1] This organisation is in the process of revising its guidelines, including the above article. It remains to be seen what consensus will emerge within the academy on this question.

We believe that there is a close relationship between society's wish for suicide to be an option for terminal-phase patients and collective misconceptions about the pain experienced by these patients. A better theoretical knowledge of the mechanisms of pain and better pain management could help, if not to calm the debate, then at least to make it more rational and focused.[2]

That being said, it should not be thought that the perspectives offered by palliative medicine will automatically remove all pertinence from the debate on voluntary death or assisted suicide.[3] In reality, this debate is based on a demand which is certainly inspired by the moral imperative to fight pain, but which also, and more importantly, considers that expression of an individual's autonomy should not be restricted by society's common values. In essence, this is not simply a debate on the practical arrangements for practising end-of-life medicine, but a philosophical and religious debate which is ongoing and to which a perfect response will not be found solely on the basis of medical practice and law.

1.
"Assistance au décès", item 2.2.

2.
For a presentation of palliative medicine in Switzerland, see especially: Rapin, C.-H., *Fin de vie: nouvelles perspectives pour les soins palliatifs*, Payot, Lausanne, 1989; and the newsletter *Info-Kara*, published by the Swiss Society of Palliative Medicine and the IUGG Documentation Centre on Palliative Care.

3.
On the ethical implications of palliative medicine, see Bondolfi, A., "Abschied nehmen ohne Qual: zum Vehältnis zwischen palliativer Medizin und Ethik", in La stagione degli addii, as well as Malacrida, R. and Martignoni, G., *The season of goodbyes*, Ed. Alice, Comano, 1991, pp. 96-101.

United Kingdom – The illegality of euthanasia

by Sheila McLean

Put simply, euthanasia is illegal in the United Kingdom. Thus, whether it is voluntary, non-voluntary or involuntary[1] it is a criminal offence to participate in actively assisting the death of another person. However, as will become clear, there is some confusion about precisely what is encompassed by the term "euthanasia" although the subject has generated considerable parliamentary activity over the last few years.

In order to avoid perpetuating any confusion, it is worth at this point clarifying what is meant by euthanasia in the context of this chapter. Euthanasia is taken to mean the active taking of a life at the express request of the individual. Although technically this could arise in any situation, since consent is not generally a defence in the criminal law, the debate about voluntary euthanasia is generally conducted within the constraints of the doctor-patient relationship, which has been held to be different from other relationships in this sense.[2] Thus, for example, I do not decriminalise an assault (with, of course, the exception of rape[3]) by agreeing to it;[4] I can, however, accept surgery – which is also technically an assault – by authorising the surgeon to carry it out. Euthanasia may also be carried out passively, but it is here that much of the confusion, which will be referred to below, is generated.

Assisted suicide

Before considering this further it is, however, worth also noting what euthanasia is not. There is, for example, a clear difference between euthanasia and assisted suicide; a distinction which is established in legislation in England and Wales although not in Scotland. In euthanasia, a third party actually carries out the killing; in assisted suicide the patient carries out the final act, although the means to do this are provided by the third party, usually a doctor. In England and Wales, Section 2 of the Suicide Act 1961 prohibits anyone from assisting in the suicide of

1.
To use the distinction made by Glover, J., *Causing death and saving lives*, Penguin, Harmondsworth, 1977 (reprinted 1984).

2.
See Lord Mustill in R. v. Brown [1993] 2 All ER 75.

3.
This is because absence of consent is central to the crime.

4.
R. v. Donovan [1934] 2 KB 498; see also R. v Brown, quoted above; and Laskey, Jaggard and Brown v. the United Kingdom, (1997) 24 EHRR 39.

another person, and from time to time cases come before the courts. Most recently, the issue was raised in the case of Pretty v. the United Kingdom.[1]

In this case, Dianne Pretty was suffering from motor neurone disease, a debilitating condition which meant that she was steadily losing control of her vital functions, even though she remained intellectually intact. Having failed to convince the UK courts to require the Director of Public Prosecutions (DPP) to grant her husband immunity should he assist in her suicide, her case finally reached the European Court of Human Rights. Ms Pretty claimed that a number of articles of the European Convention on Human Rights (specifically Articles 2, 3, 8, 9, and/or 14), incorporated into UK law by the Human Rights Act 1998, either required the DPP to give such an undertaking or alternatively that Section 2, sub-section 1, of the Suicide Act was incompatible with the ECHR. Had the former claim been accepted, this would have been of interest throughout the United Kingdom; the latter would only have affected England and Wales. In the event, the Court concluded that her Convention rights were not breached by the terms of the 1961 Suicide Act, and also that the DPP did not breach her rights by refusing to give the requested undertaking. This case has clear parallels with the Canadian case of Rodriguez v. A.-G. of British Columbia[2] in which the Canadian Supreme Court declined (albeit by a very small majority) to declare that the Charter of Rights and Freedoms gave individuals a right to assistance in their death.

Refusal of life preserving treatment

Nor is euthanasia the same as the patient's acknowledged right to refuse medical treatment, even although it is clear law that a person (such as a doctor) who has a duty of care is equally liable for their omissions as for their acts. Thus, arguably, if consent to the action of killing cannot render it lawful, it is unclear why consent to removal or withholding of treatment can, apparently, have just that effect. However, the distinction is one clearly recognised by law, and this was recently reinforced in the UK by the case of Ms B v. An NHS Hospital Trust.[3]

1.
(2002)66 BMLR 147.

2.
(1993) 107 DLR (4th) 342.

3.
[2002] Lloyd's Rep Med 265.

In this case, a woman had executed an advance directive following a haemorrhage in her spinal column in 1999. In 2001, she was readmitted to hospital; her condition had deteriorated and she had become tetraplegic, requiring ventilation. Although her doctors were aware of the advance directive, they did not believe that it was strictly applicable in the circumstances and declined to follow its terms. Ms B indicated in a contemporaneous statement that she wished the ventilator to be removed, whereupon the hospital arranged for a number of psychiatric evaluations to be undertaken. These opinions varied as to her mental capacity, but finally she was held to be competent. She executed a second advance directive, but again her doctors were unwilling to carry out her repeated wishes – including contemporaneous wishes – for the ventilator to be removed.

Dame Butler-Sloss, President of the Family Division, heard Ms B's case, and concluded that Ms B was indeed competent to make health care decisions and therefore, like all patients, she had a right to refuse even life preserving treatment. Two elements of the decision are of particular interest. In the case of euthanasia, it is often argued that a person asking for death is mentally disturbed or even ill. In debate in the House of Lords on this topic, for example, the Lord Bishop of Oxford expressed a perception which is shared by many that:

> "The request to die indicates that something is wrong. Let us concentrate on identifying what is wrong and doing all we can to make it right."[1]

Ubel also points to the difficulties associated with assessing the state of mind of the person seeking death, pointing out that:

> "Psychiatric diagnoses depend, in part, on lists of behaviours and thoughts. In some diagnoses, feelings of helplessness and suicidal ideation are criteria for mental illness. This creates a circular chain of diagnostic proof: 'Desiring suicide is a form of mental illness. Mental illness prevents people from being rational. Therefore, desiring suicide is not rational.'"[2]

In the case of Ms B, it can be speculated that doubts about the "rightness" of her decision at least in part informed the

1.
Hansard, 6 May 1998, Column 716 (HL).

2.
Ubel, P.A.., "Assisted suicide and the case of Dr Quill and Diane", Issues in Law and Medicine, Vol. 8, No. 4, 1993, pp. 487 and 498.

1.
Ibid., p. 281.

2.
Id.

3.
(1993) 12 BMLR 64,
p. 137.

4.
For the position in the
UK, see McLean,
S.A.M. and Britton,
A., *Sometimes a Small
Victory*, Institute of
Law and Ethics in
Medicine, Glasgow
University, 1996; an
example of the posi-
tion elsewhere can be
found in Zinn, C., "A
third of surgeons in
New South Wales
admit to euthanasia",
*British Medical Jour-
nal*, 323, 2001,
p. 1268; Meier, D.E.,
Emmons, C.-A.,
Wallenstein, S. et al.,
"A national survey of
physician-assisted sui-
cide and euthanasia in
the United States",
*New England Journal
of Medicine*, 338,
1998, p. 1193; for a
brief discussion of
prosecutions in the
UK, see Mason, J.K.,
McCall Smith, R.A.
and Laurie, G.T., *Law
and Medical Ethics*,
6th edition, Butter-
worths, London,
2002, paragraphs
18.4 et seq.

5.
Mason, McCall Smith
and Laurie, op. cit.,
paragraph 18.6.

6.
R. v. Cox (1992) 12
BMLR 38.

psychiatric diagnoses which declared her to be incompetent. Dame Butler-Sloss, however, firmly reminded us that:

"There is a presumption that a patient has the mental capacity to make decisions whether to consent to or refuse medical treatment offered to him or her."[2]

Thus, it is for those who dispute this to establish it; not the other way round. Secondly, she reminded health care providers that:

"[...] a seriously disabled patient who is mentally competent has the same right to personal autonomy and to make deci-sions as any other person with mental capacity."[2]

Active euthanasia

Active euthanasia is the deliberate killing of a person, at their request. As has been said, this is technically illegal in the United Kingdom, and would be charged as murder or manslaughter (culpable homicide in Scotland). Lord Mustill made this very clear in the case of Airedale NHS Trust v. Bland when he said:

"[T]hat 'mercy killing' by active means is murder [...] has never as far as I know been doubted. The fact that the doctor's motives are kindly will for some, although not for all, transform the moral quality of his act, but this makes no difference in law. It is intent to kill or cause grievous bodily harm which consti-tutes the *mens rea* of murder, and the reason why the intent was formed makes no difference at all."[3]

Despite the apparent clarity of the law, and despite the evi-dence that doctors are involved in the death of their patients, even although it is against the law,[4] prosecutions are seldom brought, and when they are, there is a "reluctance of British juries to convict a medical practitioner of serious crime when the charge arises from what they see as his considered medical judgment".[5]

Perhaps the most important prosecution was that brought against Dr Cox in 1992.[6] In this case, Dr Cox injected his patient with potassium chloride and entered this into the medical notes. As this substance has no direct therapeutic benefit, it seemed clear that Dr Cox's intention was to kill his elderly patient, whose pain was so dreadful that she had repeatedly asked for deliverance. The patient, Mrs Lillian Boyes, was suffering from rheumatoid arthritis; an extremely painful but not terminal condition. Dr Cox was eventually convicted of attempted murder.

The conviction of Dr Cox was unusual, as has been suggested above, but speculatively it may have resulted from the nature of the substance he selected. Potassium chloride is not widely used as an analgesic; indeed, the likely effect of injecting this will be the virtually instant death of the patient. This meant, therefore, that Dr Cox could not easily avail himself of the one defence that he might have had; namely, the doctrine of double effect. Briefly, this doctrine – which was first accepted in the English courts in the case of R. v. Adams[1] – allows that an act which has a bad outcome (such as death) will not be penalised so long as its intention was to achieve a good end (namely the alleviation of suffering). Thus, the judge in R. v. Cox made it clear that:

> "If a doctor genuinely believes that a certain course is beneficial to his patient, either therapeutically or analgesically, even though he recognises that that course carries with it a risk to life, he is fully entitled, none the less to pursue it. If in those circumstances the patient dies, nobody could possibly suggest in that situation the doctor was guilty of murder or attempted murder."[2]

Starkly, the question of the difference between intention and foreseeability which the Adams judgment draws was before the English courts recently in the case of Re A (children)(conjoined twins: surgical separation).[3] In this case, the courts were faced with the terrible dilemma of deciding whether or not it would be lawful to permit the surgical separation of Siamese twins, in the knowledge that the inevitable outcome would be the death of one of them. Manifestly, the double effect principle was not available in these circumstances; nor was it possible, in the eyes of some judges, to decide the case on the basis of another much used device – that of "best interests". The words of Lord Justice Ward are worthy of repetition as they go to the heart of the euthanasia dilemma:

> "It should not need stating that the court cannot approve of a course of action which may be unlawful [...]. A patent in

1.
[1957] Crim. LR 365.

2.
Ibid., p. 41.

3.
(2000) 57 BMLR 1.

terminal decline, racked with pain which treatment may not be able fully to alleviate, may beg to die and it may be said – at least by some – that it is in his best interests that he should be allowed so to do, but that would not justify unlawfully killing him."[1]

Passive euthanasia

This category is rather more difficult to describe, and it is perhaps for this reason that the confusion alluded to earlier has occasionally arisen. Causing death passively can take a number of forms, and can arise in a number of situations in which very different views and opinions can arise. Most commonly, of course, passive killing arises where a decision is taken to withhold or withdraw medical treatment. Some commentators have suggested that in fact this is very different from euthanasia. In a parliamentary debate in 1995, for example, the then Permanent Under-Secretary of State for Health said:

> "It is essential to draw a clear distinction between euthanasia, which is a positive intervention to end life, and the with-holding or withdrawal of treatment that has no curative or beneficial effect. The question of whether to withhold treatment from someone who is not benefiting from it is different from euthanasia, although it raises similar moral and ethical questions."[2]

Still others, however, would suggest that failure to provide life preserving medical treatment is morally and legally equivalent to active euthanasia and therefore is justifiably considered under the heading of euthanasia. Indeed, the Minister's comments do not in fact distinguish the two; rather they assert the difference and then concede the relative similarities. Of course there are circumstances when it is clear that medical treatment is futile. Its absence, then, will not affect the outcome of the patients' condition. With or without treatment, they will not recover. This being the case, to provide the treatment could be said to be both inhumane and an assault on the patient. Few would dispute the propriety of such decisions, based as they are on a clinical judgment about the value of treatment. However, this has raised the question of what amounts to

1.
Ibid., p. 43.

2.
Tom Sackville, *Hansard*, 19 April 1995, Column 168.

"treatment" for these purposes. In the United Kingdom, much of the debate has focused on the withholding or withdrawing of nutrition and hydration, following the cases of Airedale NHS Trust v. Bland[1] and Law Hospital NHS Trust v. Lord Advocate.[2]

In both cases, it was held (at least by a number of the judges) that nutrition and hydration could be considered as medical treatment (a view with which the British Medical Association is in agreement)[3] in circumstances where it is delivered artificially and there is no hope of recovery. Each of these cases involved patients in a persistent (or permanent) vegetative state, and in each case the superior courts permitted withdrawal of assisted nutrition and hydration, with the result that the patient died. More recently, in the case of NHS Trust A v. Mrs M, NHS Trust B v. Mrs H,[4] the judgment in Bland was upheld, and – most importantly – it was held that withdrawing nutrition and hydration did not (in appropriate circumstances) breach the protections offered by the terms of the European Convention on Human Rights.

The apparent acceptance that assisted nutrition and hydration can amount to medical treatment has not been uncontroversial and at least two attempts have been made in the UK Parliament specifically to insist that their withdrawal should amount to a criminal offence.[5] In December 2002, a petition signed by some 93 000 people was presented to parliament urging the government "to introduce without delay proposals for legislation which outlaws the withdrawal of food and fluid (however delivered) with the purpose or intention of causing death by omission".[6] Finally, an Early Day Motion[7] was laid down on 8 January 2003, calling on the government to withdraw a document entitled "Making decisions: helping people who have difficulty deciding for themselves", which incorporates the distinction relating to nutrition and hydration.

Distinctions and differences?

Space does not permit thorough discussion of the other areas in which end-of-life decisions may be taken, for example in the case of advance directives or statements. However, it is worth

1.
(1993) 12 BMLR 64.

2.
(1996) 39 BMLR 166.

3.
Withholding and Prolonging Life-Prolonging Medical Treatment: Guidance for Decisions Makers, 2nd edition, BMJ Books, London, 2001.

4.
(2001) 58 BMLR 87.

5.
Medical Treatment (Prevention of Euthanasia) Bill (House of Commons, session 1999/2000); Patient's Protection Bill (House of Lords, session 2001/2003). Broadly, these bills encapsulate the same offence: "It shall be unlawful for any person responsible for the care of a patient to withdraw or withhold from the patient medical treatment or sustenance if his purpose or one of his purposes in doing so is to hasten or otherwise cause the death of the patient."

6.
Hansard, 10 December 2002 (House of Commons).

7.
This is a parliamentary device which simply notifies parliament of interest in a particular issue, but does not anticipate that it will be debated. This particular EDM was signed by some 60 Members of Parliament.

mentioning briefly the status of such directives in UK law, which was recently clarified in the case of AK (medical treatment: consent)[1] in which a 19-year-old youth's decision that, when his motor neurone disease had progressed to the point where he had lost his ability to communicate, all ventilation, nutrition and hydration should be removed two weeks later. Essentially, the status of advance statements had already been recognised in the case of Re C (adult: refusal of treatment),[2] in which a man suffering from paranoid schizophrenia was permitted both to refuse life saving treatment and also to insist that it should not be imposed on him in the future should he become incompetent.

However, what does seem clear is that UK law remains opposed to active euthanasia, but that it will permit – in a number of situations – what might reasonably be called passive euthanasia. It has been suggested that this distinction is at best confused and at worst disingenuous.[3] Moreover, Beauchamp and Childress suggest that the rightness or wrongness of something depends:

> "[...] on the merit of the justification underlying the action, not on the type of action it is. Neither killing nor letting die, therefore, is *per se* wrongful, and in this regard they are to be distinguished from murder, which is *per se* wrong. Both killing and letting die are *prima facie* wrong, but can be justified under some circumstances."[4]

The somewhat tortuous reasoning which distinguishes between actively and passively bringing about the death of a patient – especially given, as we have seen, that a duty of care exists – has also not escaped some of the most senior judges in the United Kingdom. In the case of Airedale NHS Trust v. Bland, already referred to, Lord Mustill noted that "[t]he conclusions that the declaration [that nutrition and hydration could be removed] can be upheld depends crucially on a distinction drawn by the criminal law between actions and omissions [...]".[5] He continued:

> "The acute unease which I feel about adopting this way through the legal and ethical maze is I believe due in an important part to the sensation that however much the

1.
(2001) 58 BMLR 151.

2.
[1994] 1 All ER 819.

3.
McLean, S.A.M., "Law at the end of life – What next", in McLean, S.A.M. (ed.), *Death, Dying and the Law*, Dartmouth, 1996.

4.
Beauchamp, T.L. and Childress, J.S., *Principles of biomedical ethics*, 4th edition, OUP, Oxford, 1994, p. 225.

5.
(1993) 12 BMLR 64, p. 132.

terminologies may differ, the ethical status of the two courses of action is for all relevant purposes indistinguishable. By dismissing this appeal I fear that your Lordships' House may only emphasise the distortions of a legal structure which is already both morally and intellectually misshapen."[1]

In the same case, Lord Browne-Wilkinson also noted that it was not possible to use the distinction sometimes drawn between foreseeability and intention. As he said, "[...] the whole purpose of stopping artificial feeding is to bring about the death of Anthony Bland".[2] None the less, authority was ultimately given for the removal of the nutrition and hydration, and Anthony Bland subsequently died.

UK law, therefore, would seem explicitly to draw distinctions which are open to challenge. It is clear that there is little political will to review the prohibition on active euthanasia, even following a major investigation in the House of Lords in 1994,[3] whose major conclusion on this was firmly backed by the government.[4] The House of Lords said unequivocally:[4].

"[...] we do not believe that these arguments [those prioritising patient choice] are sufficient reasons to weaken society's prohibition of intentional killing. That prohibition is the cornerstone of law and social relationships. It protects each one of us impartially, embodying the belief that all are equal. We do not wish that protection to be diminished and we therefore recommend that there should be no change in the law to permit euthanasia."[5]

Mason, McCall Smith and Laurie conclude that "[t]he chances of legislation which legalises active euthanasia being accepted in the United Kingdom are very slim [...]".[6] In this, one suspects, they are correct, despite the fact that opinion evidence (albeit therefore anecdotal) suggests consistently that a majority of the population would like to see euthanasia (and assisted suicide) legalised.[7] Indeed, there is some evidence that attitudes amongst doctors are also moving in that direction,[8] although this must be seen as ambivalent, and is certainly not British Medical Association policy.

1.
Ibid.

2.
Ibid., p. 127.

3.
"Report of the Select Committee on Medical Ethics" (HL Paper 21-1, 1994).

4.
Cmnd 2553/1994.

5.
Paragraph 237.

6.
Mason, McCall Smith and Laurie, op. cit., paragraph 18.22.

7.
See McLean and Britton, op. cit; and Wise, J., "Public supports euthanasia for most desperate cases", *British Medical Journal*, 313, 1996, p. 1423.

8.
McLean and Britton, op. cit; but see Coulson, J., "Doctors oppose legal mercy killing for dying", *BMA News Review*, 15 March 1995.

1.
Hansard, 22 May 2002, Column 73WH (House of Commons).

2.
Dworkin, R., *Life's dominion*, Harper Collins, London, 1993, p. 217.

3.
Harris, J., "Euthanasia and the value of life", in Keown, J. (ed.), *Euthanasia examined: ethical, clinical and legal perspectives*, Cambridge University Press, Cambridge, 1995, pp. 6, 10 (cit.).

4.
Fletcher, J., "The courts and euthanasia", *Law, Medicine and Health Care*, Vol. 15, 4, winter 1987-88, pp. 223, 226 (cit.).

5.
Established under the Scotland Act 1998.

6.
As was affirmed by Yvette Cooper MP, in House of Commons Standing Committee C (Pt 4), and Ann Winterton MP, "The Scotland Act 1998 gave jurisdiction over almost all aspects of criminal law in Scotland to the Holyrood Parliament".

In fact, legal activity in the UK Parliament has tended in recent years to focus on narrowing rather than expanding the range of permissible end-of-life decisions. What is clear, however, is that parliament wishes to retain for itself the authority to set the agenda and decide what is and what is not legal. In the Bland case, it was stated by a number of judges that it was for parliament and not the courts to pronounce on this matter, and this has been greeted enthusiastically by some Members of Parliament who fear that court decisions, such as those in Bland and NHS Trust A v. Mrs M, NHS Trust B v. Mrs H, are introducing euthanasia by the back door. Equally, they fear that the decision is being taken out of the hands of parliament and is being given to the courts or the regulators of medicine, such as the BMA and the General Medical Council. One MP, for example, has said, "[i]t is not good enough that parliament has not had the opportunity to debate who should be given the onerous task of deciding who should live and who should die"[1]

The taboo that surrounds intentional deprivation of life seems, therefore, to remain powerful in the United Kingdom, despite the voices raised in favour of legalisation. Dworkin, for example, has said that "[m]aking someone die in a way that others approve, but he believes a horrifying contradiction of his life, is a devastating, odious form of tyranny".[2] And Harris proposes that:

> "If the harm of ending a life is principally a harm to the individual whose life it is, and if this harm must in turn be understood principally as the harm of depriving that individual of something that they value and want, then voluntary euthanasia will not be wrong on this account."[3]

It may be that Fletcher is right; that "[w]hat it comes down to is that most people, including the courts, want the end – death – in certain tragic situations, but that the taboo forbids the means".[4] It certainly appears that law reform in the Westminster Parliament is unlikely, although it should be borne in mind that the Scottish Parliament[6] has authority over the criminal law, meaning that Scotland could legislate to legalise euthanasia irrespective of the position in England, Wales and Northern Ireland.[7] It has to be said, however, that this seems equally unlikely, although it remains a theoretical possibility.

United States – Euthanasia, assisted suicide and the "right to die"

by Lois Snyder[1]

Euthanasia, assisted suicide and, particularly, physician-assisted suicide have been the subjects of much debate in the United States. These topics raise issues of great importance for society and the medical profession, and interest in them has grown alongside patient concerns and fears about the inadequacy of end-of-life health care. Euthanasia is not legal in the United States. Physician-assisted suicide is currently legal only in the state of Oregon. Implementation of Oregon's law continues to prompt debate about this form of assisted suicide.

Yet, despite years of discussion, the theoretical and practical parameters of assisted suicide and euthanasia are often unclear. Sometimes the phrase "the right to die" has been invoked to describe the debate around death and dying. But that phrase is really an overstatement, delineating a much broader right then is actually found in American law.

Currently, there is no positive "right" to do something or having something done to you to bring on death in the United States. What does exist is a right to refuse treatment, including life sustaining treatment. And, for the past few years, physician-assisted suicide has been legal in one state. But none of this has conferred a "right" to die and, in fact, the right to refuse treatment, including that which may result in death, has been distinguished repeatedly from assisted suicide, physician-assisted suicide and euthanasia, clinically, ethically and legally.

Words are important in these debates. It has been noted that the Dutch have used the phrase "medical decisions at the end of life" to include physician-assisted suicide and euthanasia, emphasising the point of view that these are decisions within the purview of the medical encounter (Thomasma, 1996). Many disagree with this formulation. The Oregon Death with Dignity Act specifically says that actions taken in accordance with it "shall not for any purpose constitute suicide, assisted suicide, mercy killing or homicide, under the law". Instead, the individual is obtaining "medication to end his or her life in a

1.
The views expressed here are those of the author, not necessarily of the American College of Physicians.

humane and dignified matter".[1] These approaches lend confusion to the debate. Another approach is to be clear about the acts, purposes, intentions and implications at issue here. This is especially so because suicide and, particularly, assisted suicide are social acts with implications for the community and society, as well as for individuals and their families. Physician-assisted suicide, when legalised, becomes a new social service (Byock, 1997).

So, a brief review of definitions is in order. Assisted suicide is the act of providing help to an individual to end his or her life. Most of the American debate has revolved around assisted suicide as physician-assisted suicide. Physician-assisted suicide involves the participation of a physician in the provision, but not the direct administration, of the medical means to help an individual take his or her own life. This usually means taking a lethal dosage of medication prescribed by a physician for that purpose. It does not mean the withholding or withdrawal of life sustaining medical care, based on patient refusal of treatment. Physician-assisted suicide is also distinguishable from euthanasia, where the physician performs an act he or she specifically intends to end life. Lethal injection is the common example of euthanasia (Snyder and Caplan, 1996).

The terms above will be used in this article. As an ethical matter, and clinically as well, it is important to try to clarify the differences between these practices. Terms, such as "aid-in-dying" or "physician-assisted death" or "right to die", that lump together categories and ignore legal distinctions can cloud the ethics of what is at stake for patients, vulnerable populations, end-of-life health care, the medical profession and society.

Suicide and attempted suicide are no longer illegal in the United States. Mental health law governs this area, not criminal codes. However, American society has sought to prevent suicide, through involuntary hospitalisation procedures and other measures. Assisting a suicide has remained a specific statutory offence in most states. Suicide is the eighth leading cause of death in the United States, and occurs most among the elderly and the young (New York State Task Force on Life and the Law, 1994).

1.
Oregon Death with Dignity Act, Oregon Revised Statutes, 127.800-127.897.

Why do people want the option of assisted suicide when seriously ill? Some individuals want more control over the process of dying. Some fear pain or a protracted death involving unwanted respirators, feeding tubes and other technology. Many individuals who desire suicide are depressed (Block, 2000; Baile et al., 1993) and especially among terminally ill patients, the wish is often not stable over time (Chochinov et al., 1995; Chochinov et al., 1999). Some regret having watched loved ones die of a terminal illness without effective pain and symptom control and are also concerned they will not receive good care when they need it (Buchan and Tolle, 1995; Foley, 1991). Many are concerned about becoming a burden on their families or ending their days in a nursing home. Loss of dignity is feared.

Providing good end-of-life care is an ethical duty of the medical profession (American College of Physicians Ethics Manual, 1998). Physicians should honour patient refusals of treatment according to now well-established ethical, clinical and legal standards for the withholding or withdrawal of medical interventions. Good pain control should be a priority (Abraham, 1999). But the state of end-of-life care in the United States is lacking according to the Institute of Medicine Report, "Approaching death: improving care at the end of life" (Field and Cassel, 1997). The $28 million SUPPORT project[1] (Phillips et al., 2000) also provided evidence that Americans are not dying well. SUPPORT documented inadequate pain control, unwanted aggressive treatment at the end of life and problems in patient-physician communication (SUPPORT Principle Investigators, 1995).

In this context, then, it is not surprising that the option of physician-assisted suicide is seen as desirable by some. After much battling, it is now legal in the state of Oregon.

The Oregon experience

The Oregon Death with Dignity Act was first passed by voters as a citizens' initiative in 1994 (51% to 49%). It legalised physician-assisted suicide under detailed procedures. Implementation

1.
Study to understand Prognoses and Preferences for Outcomes and Risks of Treatment.

was initially delayed by legal action challenging the law and then an attempt to appeal the law.

A terminally ill Oregonian who is mentally capable as judged by two physicians can get a prescription for medication to end his or her life in a humane and dignified manner if they make the numerous oral and written requests within certain time periods and using a form contained in the act or substantially similar to it. The physician who complies with the request must:

1. determine if the patient is terminal, capable and has voluntarily made the request;

2. inform the patient of the medical diagnosis, prognosis, potential risks of taking the medication to be prescribed, probable result of taking the drugs, and the feasible alternatives including, but not limited to, comfort care, hospice care and pain control;

3. refer the patient to a consulting physician for medical confirmation of the diagnosis and a determination that the patient is capable and acting voluntarily;

4. refer the patient for counselling if appropriate;

5. request that the patient notify next of kin;

6. inform the patient he or she has the opportunity to rescind the request at any time and offer the patient the opportunity to do so at the end of a fifteen-day waiting period following the initial oral request;

7. verify immediately prior to writing the prescription that the patient is making an informed decision;

8. document all of this in the medical record;

9. ensure that all appropriate steps are carried out in accordance with the act; and

10. comply with information collection requirements of the Health Division.[1]

Data from the first four years of implementation of the Oregon law has been published, but the relatively small number of documented cases prompts some to wonder if all cases are being reported. One hundred and forty people were reported to have received prescriptions for lethal doses of medication

1.
Oregon Death with Dignity Act, Oregon Revised Statutes 127.800-127.897.

from physicians under the Oregon law. A total of ninety-one deaths by physician-assisted suicide were reported and those individuals were mostly cancer patients. Some 78% of the ninety-one patients were in hospice programmes. Death by physician-assisted suicide accounted for approximately 6-9/10 000 deaths per year in the state (Ganzini et al., 2002). Interestingly, the decision to seek physician-assisted suicide was more often associated with concerns about loss of autonomy and a desire to control the circumstances of death, not because of pain, or fear of pain or suffering (Ganzini et al., 2002; Chin et al., 1999; Sullivan et al., 2000; Hedberg et al., 2002).

The Oregon law has been credited with bringing more attention to end-of-life care issues in that state. Improvements in care have been cited, including more frequent advance care planning, the lowest rate of in-hospital deaths in the country, and gains in pain management (Hedberg et al., 2002). Some researchers suggest that it may be improvements in hospice care, in part, that may explain why the rate of assisted suicide has been low overall among hospice patients (Ganzini et al., 2002).

Once again, the Oregon law is being legally challenged. The United States Attorney General has said that the use of controlled substances for the purpose of physician-assisted suicide in Oregon is not a "legitimate medical purpose" under the federal Controlled Substances Act (Steinbrook, 2002).

Refusal of treatment versus physician-assisted suicide: different acts?

Physician-assisted suicide and euthanasia have long been prohibited by medical codes of ethics. They have been seen as violations of the ethical precepts of non-maleficence (the duty to do no harm to patients) and of beneficence (the obligation to do good and to act in the best interests of the patient). Pronouncements against active steps to hasten death date back to the Hippocratic Oath and have formed the ethical core for professional opposition to these practices (Hippocrates, 1923b). Some, however, argue that the Hippocratic articulation of values allows for varied interpretations (Momeyer, 2000).

There has long been agreement, however, that stopping treatment when patients are "overmastered by disease" (Hippocrates, 1923a) is ethical and appropriate.

Today, American patients have the right to refuse treatment, including life sustaining treatment. This is based on a weighing of patient autonomy and self-determination interests against societal interests. It is not, however, a "right to die". What has been established to date, and the ethical principles that underpin it, are about protecting an individual's interest in bodily integrity and right to be left alone – not a right to something.

The withholding or withdrawing of life sustaining treatment based on patient wishes has been ethically, legally and clinically distinguished from physician-assisted suicide and euthanasia (Sulmasy, 1998). State courts and the US Supreme Court[1] have consistently made these distinctions.

In two decisions in July 1997, the Supreme Court ruled that there is no constitutional right to assisted suicide.[2] The court did not find either of the lower court decisions in Compassion in Dying v. Washington[3] and Quill v. Vacco[4] to be persuasive. Instead, the court specifically distinguished refusal of treatment from physician-assisted suicide. The decision concluded that the withdrawal of treatment based on patient wishes respects a patient's right to be free of unwanted medical treatment. That act is about allowing an individual to protect him or herself from bodily intrusion. It is not a right to control the manner and time of death, or a right to secure an intervention from the physician to end one's life. While ruling that there is no constitutional right to physician-assisted suicide and that states may prohibit it, however, the court also left open the possibility that individual states could legalise it, as Oregon has done in limited circumstances.

It may be helpful to consider these issues further by looking at some examples exploring whether there is a valid distinction between assisted suicide and refusal of treatment (Miller et al., 2000). Competent individuals are used in these examples because, to date, the American movement to legalise physician-assisted suicide has stressed the right of the competent individual to assisted suicide.

1.
Cruzan v. Director, Missouri Department of Health, 110 S.Ct 2841 (1990); Vacco v. Quill, 117 S.Ct 2293 (1997); and Washington v. Glucksberg, 117 S.Ct 2258 (1997).

2.
Vacco v. Quill, op. cit. and Washington v. Glucksberg, op. cit.

3.
79 F.3d 790 (9th Cir. 1996).

4.
80 F.3d 716 (2d Cir. 1996).

In the first example, a competent patient requests barbiturates to end her life when she deems her suffering from leukaemia to be unbearable. Her doctor understands her wishes and provides the prescription. She uses the medication. This is clearly an example of physician-assisted suicide. But let us look at two more examples. How similar to or different from the first one are they? What causes death – the underlying disease or the withdrawal of care? What is the intent of the participants?

In the second example, a young woman with locked-in syndrome becomes quadriplegic and unable to speak, but feels pain and is competent. After being weaned from a ventilator, she makes it known that she wants to die and refuses artificial food and fluids, wanting only comfort care. The health care team is hesitant and recommends otherwise, but then complies.

Thirdly, a competent elderly nursing home resident is bedridden and incontinent after a number of acute medial problems. She is not dying, but wants to die based on her perceptions that her quality of life is poor. She refuses antibiotics but survives pneumonia. She then stops eating and drinking, with comfort care, and dies a few days later.

Physicians in the last two cases may be said to be letting nature take its course – that is, death is caused by the underlying disease. In all three cases the intent of the patient is to bring on death, realise self-determination and end suffering. Only the first patient is terminally ill. Physicians in the second and third cases facilitate informed and voluntary patient wishes by withdrawing life support and/or providing comfort care – but their intent is not to hasten death. Sometimes, however, intentions in end-of-life care can be very complicated or unclear.

A more fundamental dividing line may be that patient self-determination is more at stake in the treatment refusal/decision to stop eating and drinking cases, than in a request for physician-assisted suicide. To impose unwanted care is a bodily invasion, a violation of bodily integrity that does not respect patient wishes and rights. Refusing to honour a patient's request for a lethal dose of medication for use in suicide is not a bodily invasion. So while the first case is one of

1.
Cruzan c. Director, Missouri Dept. of Health, in *S.Ct*, 110, 2841, 1990; Vacco c. Quill, in *S.Ct.*, 117, 2293,1997; Washington c. Glucksberg, in *S.Ct.*, 117, 2258, 1997.

2.
Vacco c. Quill, *op.cit.*, et Washington c. Glucksberg, *op.cit.*

3.
79 F. 3d 790 (9ᵉ Cir. 1996).

4.
80 F. 3d 716 (2ᵉ Cir. 1996).

physician-assisted suicide, under this line of analysis, the second and third are not – instead, they are cases of patients exercising their right to refuse treatment (Miller et al., 2000).

On a related issue, the Supreme Court did seem to be support-ive of the use of pain medication even in doses that could hasten death, as long as the intent is to relieve pain and not to end the patient's life (Meisel et al., 2000) – lending legal sup-port to the doctrine of "double effect". A new debate has arisen over the practice known as "terminal sedation" – sedating to unconsciousness coupled with refusal of food and fluids. Some commentators prefer the terminology "sedation of the immi-nently dying". Both "camps" recognise the need for careful con-sideration of the issues and guidelines on how such practices are evaluated and administered for individual patients (Quill and Byock, 2000; Jansen and Sulmasy, 2002). This debate will likely grow.

The ethics of physician-assisted suicide: pro and con

The ethical arguments in support of physician-assisted suicide (or euthanasia) centre on the duty of physicians to relieve patient suffering and on a heightened understanding of the duty to respect patient autonomy (Snyder and Weiner, 1996). This parallels a current trend in bioethics emphasising patient autonomy, almost to the exclusion of other interests and values. Deciding to end one's life and having control over the manner and timing of death are deeply private matters which do no harm to others, it is argued, and should not be prohib-ited by the government or the medical profession (Brock, 1992; Angell, 1997). This is especially so, it is argued, given the suffering that patients can experience at the end of life – pain or nausea or other physical symptoms, depression and anxiety, dependency on others, and existential suffering, including a sense of hopelessness or loss of dignity.

Further, it is argued that trust in the patient-physician relationship is harmed when physician-assisted suicide is not an option, or an option for discussion. From this position, physician-assisted suicide is an act of compassion. It respects patient choice and enables the physician to fulfil a duty of non-abandonment (Wanzer et al., 1989; Brody, 1992). It is said to "demedicalise" death as a response to the sometimes unfettered use of high technology at the end of life.

But is it medicine's role to try to relieve all human suffering (Pellegrino, 1993)? Does physician-assisted suicide demedicalise death or medicalise suicide (Salem, 1999)? Can such a private and significant act be meaningfully regulated?

American medicine has not excelled at end-of-life care. As a profession, and as a society that has difficulty openly discussing death, we can do better at meeting patient and family needs at the end of life. But is death mostly the domain of medicine? Do not clergy members, social workers, other health professionals, family, friends and others have a role in a person's final phase of life, if desired by the individual?

Is intentionally hastening death the role of the physician? Many argue that doctors should heal and comfort, not be agents of death (Gaylin et al., 1988). Prohibitions of assisted suicide and euthanasia have a long tradition in medicine. While not absolute, a professional ethic is significant not only because of the power of the argument, but also because of its context and articulation of norms in the history of the profession (Miles, 1995). In medicine, assistance with suicide can compromise the patient-physician relationship and the trust necessary to sustain it. It can also undermine the integrity and social role of the profession, and alter the meaning of beneficence and the duty to do good and to promote the best interests of the patient (Snyder and Sulmasy, 2001; Singer and Siegler, 1990).

Society in general and the medical profession in particular have obligations to safeguard the value of human life and to protect the most vulnerable members of the community – the elderly, the disabled, the sick, the poor, minorities, and other potentially vulnerable individuals and groups. Does respect for individual autonomy trump all other values (Callahan, 1992)? Might some individuals come to believe they were a burden and view themselves as having a "duty to die" (Hardwig, 1997)?

Should there be some limits on individual autonomy? A frequently used analogy is that an individual does not have the freedom and right to make himself a slave because doing so would undermine that very freedom. Would a broad right to suicide undermine the very meaning of autonomy, which is about far more than just "control"? What are the purposes and consequences of such self-determination for the individual and for society? Ironically, should this form of self-determination require the assistance of others? Should those others be members of a healing profession?

On a practical level, concerns arise about slippery slopes. If widely legalised, could access to physician-assisted suicide be successfully restricted to the competent, terminally ill adults? What about the suffering of individuals who are not terminally ill? The individual with Alzheimer's disease who fears for the future and desires euthanasia "when the time comes" but who will lose competence? Is it discriminatory to restrict the practice to certain categories of individuals and to physician-assisted suicide (Kamisar, 1993)? Who is to judge the severity of another individual's suffering? Furthermore, practical problems exist in our ability to accurately predict how long a terminally ill patient has to live (Knaus et al., 1995)

Also on a practical level, there is potential for abuse, especially in the current health care environment of cost containment (Wolf, 1996). Guidelines and regulatory safeguards have been proposed (Miller et al., 1994; Hellig et al., 1997; Young et al., 1997). A task force in Oregon produced a guidebook for health care providers implementing the Oregon Death with Dignity Act (Task Force to Improve the Care of Terminally Ill Oregonians, 1998). But some question whether proposed guidelines have been or can ever be effective (Coleman and Fleischman, 1996).

Further, many patients do not have a long-standing relationship with a physician who knows them well. Is not this important if there is to be a meaningful discussion about, and voluntary informed consent to, physician-assisted suicide?

American society and the medical profession are divided on whether to legalise physician-assisted suicide and euthanasia

(Gillespie, 1999). Some physicians support the legalisation of assisted suicide (Bachman et al., 1996; Back et al., 1996; Emmanuel et al., 1996; Ezekiel et al., 2000; Lee et al., 1996; Shapiro et al., 1994) although may not themselves be willing to participate. Oregon has legalised physician-assisted suicide and is generating some data about its experience. Assisting a suicide remains a specific statutory offence in most states and euthanasia is still illegal everywhere in the United States.

The debate about physician-assisted suicide is a defining one for American medicine and society. In the United States, there is no general "right" to health care. There is a right to refuse treatment. Should the next logical step be a right to assisted suicide or euthanasia?

To some degree, we arrive at these issues because of inadequacies in the state of palliative care and our ability to provide comfort and compassion at the end of life. Health care providers, among others, can do a better job of caring for, meeting the needs of, and demonstrating support for those who would see suicide as their best option. Requests for physician-assisted suicide should be an opportunity to explore and address the patient's concerns and maximise the tools of palliative care, including hospice and good pain management (Snyder and Sulmasy, 2001). Some physicians may undertreat pain for fear of respiratory suppression, even though this usually does not result (Fohr, 1998). And there is strong ethical support for increasing pain medications in terminal illness when the intent is to relieve pain, even if this may also shorten life (Sulmasy, 1999). Physician and patient should discuss and understand the goals of treatment and search for the least harmful care alternatives. Physician-assisted suicide is legal in Oregon. But improvements in end-of-life care in the United States have really just begun.

References

Abraham, J.L. (for the ACP-ASIM End-of-Life Care Consensus Panel), "Management of pain and spinal cord compression in patients with advanced cancer", *Ann Intern Med*, 131, 1999, pp. 37-46.

American College of Physicians Ethics Manual (fourth edition), *Ann Intern Med*, 128, 1998, pp. 576-94.

Angell, M., "The Supreme Court and physician-assisted suicide – The ultimate right", *N Engl J Med*, 336, 1997, pp. 50-53.

Bachman, J.G., Alcser, K.H., Doukas, D.J., Lichtenstein, R.L., Corning, A.D. and Brody, H., "Attitudes of Michigan physicians and the public toward legalizing physician-assisted suicide and voluntary euthanasia", *N Engl J Med*, 334, 1996, pp. 303-309.

Back, A.L., Wallace, J.I., Starks, H.E. and Pearlman, R.A, "Physician-assisted suicide and euthanasia in Washington state: patient requests and physician responses", *J Am Med Assoc,* 275, 1996, pp. 919-925.

Baile, W.F., DiMaggio, J.R., Schapira, D.V. and Janofsky, J.S., "The request for assistance in dying: the need for psychiatric consultation", *Cancer*, 72, 1993, pp. 2786-2791.

Block, S.D. (for the ACP-ASIM End-of-Life Care Consensus Panel), "Assessing and managing depression in the terminally ill patient", *Ann Intern Med*, 132, 2000, pp. 209-18.

Brock, D.W., "Euthanasia", *Yale J Biol Med*, 65, 2, March-April 1992, pp. 121-9.

Brody, H., "Assisted death – A compassionate response to a medical failure", *N Engl J Med*, 327, 1992, pp. 1384-1388.

Buchan, M.L. and Tolle, S.W., "Pain relief for dying persons: dealing with physicians' fears and concerns", *J Clin Ethics*, 6, 1995, pp. 53-61.

Byock, I., "Physician-assisted suicide is not an acceptable practice", in Weir, R.F. (ed.), *Physician-assisted suicide*, University of Indiana Press, Bloomington, 1997, pp. 107-135.

Callahan, D., "When self-determination runs amok", *Hastings Cent Rep*, 22, March-April, 1992, pp. 52-55.

Chin, A.E., Hedberg, K., Higginson, G.K. and Fleming, D.W., "Legalized physician-assisted suicide in Oregon – The first year's experience", *N Engl J Med*, 340, 1999, pp. 577-583.

Chochinov, H.M., Tatryn, D., Clinch, J.J. and Dudgeon, D., "Will to live in the terminally ill", *Lancet*, 354, 1999, pp. 816-819.

Chochinov, H.M., Wilson, K., Enns, M., Mowchun, N., Lander, S., Levitt, M. and Clinch, J.J., "Desire for death in the terminally ill", *Am J Psychiatry*, 152, 1995, pp. 1185-1191.

Coleman, C.H. and Fleischman, A.R., "Guidelines for physician-assisted suicide: can the challenge be met?", *J Law Med Eth*, 24, 1996, pp. 217-224.

Emanuel, E.J., Fairclough, D.L., Daniels, E.R. and Clarridge, B.R., "Euthanasia and physician-assisted suicide: attitudes and experiences of oncology patients, oncologists, and the public", *Lancet*, 347, 1996, pp. 1805-1810.

Ezekiel, E.M., Fairclough, D., Clarridge, B.C., Blum, D., Bruera, E., Penley, W.C. et al., "Attitudes and practices of US oncologists regarding euthanasia and physician-assisted suicide", *Ann Intern Med*, 133, 2000, pp. 527-532.

Field, M.J. and Cassel, C.K. (eds.), *Approaching death: improving care at the end of life*, National Academy Press, Washington, DC, 1997.

Fohr, S.A., "The double effect of pain medication: separating myth from reality", *J Palliat Med*, 1, 1998, pp. 315-326.

Foley, K.M., "The relationship of pain and symptom management to patient requests for physician-assisted suicide", *J Pain Symptom Manage*, 6, 1991, pp. 289-297.

Ganzini, L., Harvath, T.A., Jackson, A., Goy, E.R., Miller, L.L. and Delorit, M.A., "Experiences of Oregon nurses and social workers with hospice patients who requested assistance with suicide", *N Engl J Med*, 347, 2002, pp. 582-588.

Gaylin, W., Kass, L.R., Pellegrino, E.D. and Siegle, M., "Doctors must not kill", *J Am Med Assoc*, 259, 1988, pp. 2139-2140.

Gillespie, M., *Kevorkian to face murder charges*, Gallup News Service, 19 March 1999 (www.gallup.com/poll/releases/pr990319.asp).

Hardwig, J., "Is there a duty to die?", *Hastings Cent Rep*, 27, 2, March-April, 1997, pp. 34-42.

Hedberg, K. and Tolle, S.W., "Physician-assisted suicide and changes in care of the dying: the Oregon perspective", in Snyder, L. and Caplan, A.L. (eds.), *Assisted suicide: finding common ground*, Indiana University Press, Bloomington, 2002.

Hellig, S., Brody, R., Marcus, F.S., Shavelson, L. and Sussman, P.C., "Physician-hastened death: guidelines for San Francisco Bay Area Network of Ethics Committees", *West J Med*, 166, 1997, pp. 37-78.

Hippocrates, "The art", in Jones, W.H.S. (ed.), *Hippocrates II*, Harvard University Press, Cambridge, MA, 1923a, p. 193.

Hippocrates, "The oath", in Jones W.H.S. (ed.), *Hippocrates I*, Harvard University Press, Cambridge, MA, 1923b, pp. 289-301.

Jansen, L.A. and Sulmasy, D.P., "Sedation, alimentation, hydration and equivocation: careful conversation about care at the end of life", *Ann Intern Med*, 136, 2002, pp. 845-849.

Kamisar, Y., "Are laws against assisted suicide unconstitutional?", *Hastings Cent Rep*, 23, May-June, 1993, pp. 32-41.

Knaus, W.A., Harrell, F.E., Lynn, J., Goldman, L., Phillips, R.S., Connors, A.F. et al., "The SUPPORT prognostic model: objective estimates of survival for seriously ill hospitalized adults", *Ann Intern Med,* 122, 1995, pp. 191-203.

Lee, M.A., Nelson, H.D., Tilden, V.P., Ganzini, L., Schmidt, T.A., and Tolle, S.W., "Legalizing assisted suicide – Views of physicians in Oregon", *N Engl J Med*, 334, 1996, pp. 310-315.

Meisel, A., Snyder, L., Quill, T.E., "Seven legal barriers to end-of-life care: myths, realities and grains of truth", *JAMA*, 284, 2000, pp. 2495-2501.

Miles, S.H., "Physician-assisted suicide and the profession's gyrocompass", *Hastings Cent Rep*, 25, 1995, pp. 17-19.

Miller, F., Fins, J., Snyder, L., "Assisted suicide compared with refusal of treatment: a valid distinction?", *Ann Intern Med*, 132, 2000, pp. 470-475.

Miller, F.G., Quill, T.E., Brody, H., Fletcher, J.C., Gostin, L.O. and Meier, D.E., "Regulating physician-assisted death", *N Engl J Med*, 331, 1994, pp. 119-122.

Momeyer, R., "Does physician-assisted suicide violate the integrity of medicine?", *J Med Philos*, 20, 2000, pp. 13- 24.

New York State Task Force on Life and the Law, *When death is sought: assisted suicide and euthanasia in the medical context*, Albany, New York, 1994.

Pellegrino, E.D., "Compassion needs reason too", *J Am Med Assoc*, 270, 1993, pp. 874-875.

Phillips, R.S., Hamel, M.B., Covinsky, K.E. and Lynn, J., "Findings from SUPPORT and HELP", *J Am Geriatr Soc*, 48, 2000, S1-S233.

Quill, T. and Byock, I., " Responding to intractable terminal suffering: the role of terminal sedation and voluntary refusal of food and fluids", *Ann Intern Med*, 132, 2000, pp. 408-414.

Salem, T., "Physician-assisted suicide: promoting autonomy or medicalizing suicide?", *Hastings Cent Rep*, 29, 1999, pp. 30-36.

Shapiro, R.S., Derse, A.R., Gottlieb, M., Schiedermayer, D. and Olson, M., "Willingness to perform euthanasia: a survey of physician attitudes", *Arch Intern Med*, 154, 1994, pp. 575-587.

Singer, P.A. and Siegler, M., "Euthanasia: a critique", *N Engl J Med*, 322,1990, pp. 1881-1883.

Snyder, L. and Caplan, A.L., "Die hard: end-of-life care in America", *Pa Med*, 99, 1996, pp. 10-11.

Snyder, L. and Quill, T., eds., *Physician's guide to end-of-life care*, American College of Physicians, Philadelphia, 2001.

Snyder, L. and Sulmasy D.P. for the American College of physicians, "Physician-assisted suicide", *Ann Intern Med*, 135, 2001, pp. 209-216.

Snyder, L. and Weiner, J., "Physician-assisted suicide", in Snyder L. (ed.). *Ethical choices: case studies for medical practice*, American College of Physicians, Philadelphia, 1996.

Steinbrook, R., "Physician-assisted suicide in Oregon – An uncertain future", *N Engl J Med*, 346, 2002, pp. 460-464.

Sullivan, A.D., Hedberg, K. and Fleming, D.W., "Legalized physician-assisted suicide in Oregon – The second year", *N Engl J Med*, 342, 2000, pp. 598-604.

Sulmasy, D.P., "Killing and allowing to die: another look", *J Law Med Eth*, 26, 1998, pp. 55-64.

Sulmasy, D.P. and Pellegrino, E.D., "The rule of double effect: clearing up the double talk", *Arch Intern Med*, 159, 1999, pp. 545-550.

SUPPORT Principal Investigators, "A controlled trial to improve care for seriously ill hospitalized patients", *J Am Med Assoc*, 274, 1995, pp. 1591-1598.

Task Force to Improve the Care of Terminally-Ill Oregonians, *The Oregon Death With Dignity Act: a guidebook for health care providers*, OSHU, Portland, OR, 1998.

Thomasma, D.C., "When physicians choose to participate in the death of their patient: ethics and physician-assisted suicide", *J Law Med Eth*, 24, 1996, pp. 183-197.

Wanzer, S.H., Federman, D.D., Adelstein, S.J., Cassel, C.K., Cassem, E.H., Cranford, R.E. et al., "The physician's responsibility toward hopelessly ill patients: a second look", *N Engl J Med*, 320, 1989, pp. 844-849.

Wolf, S., "Physician-assisted suicide in the context of managed care", *Duquesne Law Review*, 35, 1996, pp. 455-479.

Young, E.W., Marcus, F.S., Drought, T., Mendiola, M., Ciesielski-Carlucci, C., Alpers, A. et al., "Report of the Northern California Conference for Guidelines on Aid-in-Dying: definitions, differences, convergences, conclusions", *West J Med*, 166, 1997, pp. 381-388.

The Council of Europe
and euthanasia

Recommendation 1418 –
The position of the Council of Europe

by Dick Marty

"The vocation of the Council of Europe is to protect the dignity of all human beings and the rights which stem therefrom."

This first sentence of Recommendation 1418, "Protection of the human rights and dignity of the terminally ill and the dying", which the Council of Europe Parliamentary Assembly adopted on 25 June 1999, is one on which consensus is possible despite decades of fierce disagreement about a challenging and sensitive issue. For human dignity is invoked both by opponents of any form of euthanasia and by those who believe that, in certain well-defined circumstances, we should grant terminally ill or dying patients' insistent and carefully considered requests for their lives to be ended. In contrast, the recommendation's conclusions are uncompromising: the Committee of Ministers is asked to

> "encourage the member states of the Council of Europe to respect and protect the dignity of terminally ill or dying persons in all respects ... by upholding the prohibition against taking the life of terminally ill or dying persons, while ... recognising that a terminally ill or dying person's wish to die never constitutes any legal claim to die at the hand of another person".

This is an unambiguous position and there were legitimate grounds for thinking that it would call a halt, at least temporarily, to the lively and often impassioned debate of recent decades, both within the Parliamentary Assembly and in member states. This has not happened, as we shall see.

The Committee of Ministers replied to Recommendation 1418 in two stages. First, on 30 October 2000, it stressed the complexity of the issues and noted, regarding the absolute prohibition on intentionally taking the life of a terminally ill or dying person, that

> "the legal position differs from one member state to another on advance refusal of certain treatments and on euthanasia".

The Committee of Ministers dealt with the subject again in more detail on 26 March 2002, having previously sought the opinion of, among others, the Steering Committee for Human Rights (CDDH). The Ministers endorsed the Assembly's position about :

"upholding the prohibition against intentionally taking the life of terminally ill or dying persons",

and the principle that

"a terminally ill or dying person's wish to die cannot of itself constitute a legal justification to carry out actions intended to bring about death".

They again made the point, however, that member states had varying approaches to the issues the recommendation dealt with. They posed, but left unanswered, the question of whether states party to the European Convention on Human Rights were allowed some discretion in the matter and, if so, how much, for it accepted that, from the standpoint of the Convention, the human rights of the terminally ill and the dying posed some very complex problems of interpretation, notably regarding interplay of the various rights and freedoms.

The fact that the European Court of Human Rights has hardly ever had to rule on a euthanasia matter further complicates the Committee of Ministers' predicament, though the Court did recently deal in part with one of the questions the Ministers raised, namely whether the right to life established in Article 2 of the Convention could be interpreted as guaranteeing negative rights. The case concerned, which received prominent coverage in the world press, was that of Diane Pretty, who was terminally ill, wished to die and had asked the courts to allow her to have her life terminated. The Court of Human Rights refused her request.

"Article 2 cannot, without a distortion of language, be interpreted as conferring the diametrically opposite right, namely a right to die; nor can it create a right to self-determination in the sense of conferring on an individual the entitlement to choose death rather than life [...] The Court accordingly finds that no right to die, whether at the hands of a third person or with the assistance of a public authority, can be derived from Article 2 of the Convention.[1]

1.
Pretty v. the United Kingdom, 29 April 2002, paragraphs 39 and 40.

However, the Court has not expressed a view, either in the Pretty judgment or previously, on whether euthanasia is compatible with the Convention. Recommendation 1418 and opponents of all types of euthanasia start from the premise that Article 2 does not allow the taking of life in any circumstances. The Belgian and Dutch legislatures, after wide-ranging debate and careful thought, have come to a very different conclusion, as we shall see.

Recommendation 1418 recognises that medical technology is capable of increasingly delaying the moment of death and that, as a result, the patient as a human individual is often lost sight of. The problem posed by euthanasia has undeniably grown more acute as medicine has progressed and therapeutic techniques have become more and more sophisticated. The new technologies available to medicine often keep death at bay, less often effect a cure or ensure quality of life. This medical zealousness is often a matter of technical wizardry rather than actual benefit to the patient.

In 1976 the Parliamentary Assembly stated in Recommendation 779 that

> "the prolongation of life should not in itself constitute the exclusive aim of medical practice, which must be concerned equally with the relief of suffering".

In 1999 it was even more explicit, denouncing the "artificial prolongation of the dying process", which was felt to be a threat to the human dignity of the dying, and reiterating that

> "the obligation to respect and to protect the dignity of a terminally ill or dying person derives from the inviolability of human dignity in all stages of life".

The Assembly deplored the shortage of palliative care and good pain management and the lack or inadequacy of social and institutional support to those who wanted a peaceful leave-taking of family and friends. Appropriate care and treatment needed to be available to them, unless they chose otherwise, even if it had the possible side-effect of contributing to the shortening of the patient's life.

In its reply of 26 March 2002 the Committee of Ministers examined the problem in the light of the protection which

1.
"No one shall be subjected to torture or to inhuman or degrading treatment or punishment."

2.
Herczegfalvy v. Austria, 24 September 1992; the Court did say however that it had to satisfy itself that medical necessity had been convincingly shown to exist (paragraph 82).

3.
Ireland v. the United Kingdom, 18 January 1978 (paragraph 162).

4.
A. v. the United Kingdom, 23 September 1998 (paragraph 22).

5.
The rapporteur Ms Gatterer referred in her explanatory memorandum to the World Health Organisation definition: "the active total care of patients whose disease is not responsive to curative treatment. Control of pain, of other symptoms and of psychological, social and spiritual problems is paramount. The goal of the palliative care is achievement of the best possible quality of life for patients and their families" (see paragraph 17).

6.
Explanatory memorandum, paragraph 46.

Article 3 of the Human Rights Convention afforded to human dignity.[1] The Court stated that

"as a general rule, a measure which is a therapeutic necessity cannot be regarded as inhuman or degrading",[2]

and had also underlined that whether an act was to be classed as ill-treatment within the meaning of Article 3 depended

"on all the circumstances of the case, such as the duration of the treatment, its physical or mental effects and, in some cases, the sex, age and state of health of the victim, etc."[3]

In another judgment the Court observed that Article 3 required countries to take legislative or other measures to ensure that individuals within their jurisdiction, especially the most vulnerable – which included the terminally ill and the dying – were not subjected to inhuman or degrading treatment.[4] The Committee of Ministers again observed however that

"the dual objective of alleviating suffering whilst avoiding such violations might give rise to a wide range of national measures."

The Committee noted that, although definitions of palliative care did exist,[5] the Assembly had not attempted to define it – rightly, it commented, in view of the seeming impossibility of giving a uniform European definition of such a very broad concept. It drew attention to a European Health Committee (CDSP) study of the situation in a range of European countries which highlighted work by the Eastern and Central European Task Force on Palliative Care. A recommendation on the organisation of palliative care was adopted in November 2003 by the Committee of Ministers.

Recommendation 1418 carefully avoids using the term "euthanasia", though the concept and its problems constantly lurk in the background. The rapporteur alluded to and firmly rejected it:

"requests to health care professionals for 'mercy killing' or 'assisted suicide' were illegal and to accede to them was to contravene codes of professional ethics".[6]

The Assembly thus adopted a firmly anti-euthanasia position.[1] Palliative care and supportive end-of-life care were regarded as being of paramount importance. Patients must be given adequate assistance to ensure quality of life as far as possible. At the same time the recommendation makes it clear that terminally ill or dying persons have a right to self-determination. It recognises that patients have a right to be informed, or not to be informed if they so wish, to consult other doctors and to refuse treatment, provided that no outside influence or pressure has been exerted. It also recognises patients' right to leave advance directives or living wills refusing specific types of treatment: such directives, it says, are valid and must be complied with even when patients are incapacitated, provided their wishes are clearly expressed, they have not been swayed by any outside influence and the current illness is clearly referred to. So there is a right to self-determination, but with clear limits.

As already pointed out, the Assembly is categorical: the wishes of terminally ill or dying persons do not constitute a valid reason to take a life. There are also restrictions on refusal of treatment: a decision to refuse a specific form of treatment will be heeded only if it does not violate human dignity, and the physician still has ultimate therapeutic responsibility. In this connection the rapporteur referred to the World Medical Association's 1987 Madrid Declaration, which said that

> "deliberately ending the life of a patient, even at the patient's own request or at the request of close relatives, was unethical, though that did not preclude the physician's respecting a patient's desire for the natural process of dying to take its course in the terminal phase of sickness."[2]

But despite the Assembly's manifest hostility to any form of euthanasia, we see some inconsistencies in its position, for example in its advocacy of pain-relief "even if this treatment as a side-effect may contribute to the shortening of the individual's life"[3]. That position echoes the teaching of the Catholic Church's Catechism[4]. Surely, though, it involves euthanasia in all but name?[5] Of course the prime intention may be to alleviate suffering rather than bring about death. But is going ahead with alleviation, often in the full and certain knowledge that

1.
This position is substantially concurring with the doctrine of the Catholic Church. A Vatican note released on 16 January 2003 and signed Cardinal Josef Ratzinger denounces the "moral relativism" displayed by recent legislation on termination of pregnancy, euthanasia and homosexual unions: these are, it states, are "attacks on human life" (see *Le Monde* newspaper of 18 January 2003).

2.
Explanatory memorandum, paragraph 45.

3.
Recommendation, paragraph 9.a.vii.

4.
See Catechism, No. 2279, quoted recently by the Swiss bishops, who added: "Pope Pius XII taught that the duty of a doctor was always to alleviate the patient's sufferings, even if that might shorten life. The proper course of action is dictated by a fundamental ethical principle, that of safeguarding the dignity of a dying person, as where a doctor, without seeking to bring about death, endeavours to alleviate the sufferings of a dying person by means of palliative care whose foreseeable effect will be to bring about death (*Dying with dignity*, pastoral letter of the Swiss bishops on euthanasia and supportive care for the dying, 2002).

5.
The Swiss bishops are not afraid to use the term euthanasia: referring to "passive euthanasia" (omitting or interrupting a treatment) and "indirect active euthanasia" (treatment of symptoms and pain at the risk of shortening life), they clearly state that "in full agreement with the Swiss Academy of Medical Sciences, we consider the two forms of euthanasia mentioned as permissible and even necessary" (ibid.).

1.
4% of 250 doctors questioned during a survey carried out by the Catholic University of Milan admitted that they had actively ended the lives of dying patients. 80% admitted they had practised passive euthanasia *(Neue Zürcher Zeitung* of 13 November 2002, quoting the *Corriere della Sera* of the previous day). Earlier research points in the same direction. See B.J.Ward and P.A.Tate, "Attitudes among NHS doctors to requests for euthanasia" in the *British Medical Journal*, 1994, 308, p.1332. More recently, a highly interesting international study made as part of an EU project analysing deaths in Belgium, Denmark, the Netherlands, Italy, Sweden and Switzerland clearly showed that euthanasia is practised in a variety of ways in different countries and occurs far more frequently than might be supposed ("Medical end-of-life decision-making in six European countries", *The Lancet*, Vol. 361, 2 August 2003; see also *Bulletin des médecins suisses*, 2003, No. 32-33, p. 1676).

2.
Motion for a resolution, 4 July 2001, Doc. 9170.

death may result, really so very different from meeting the dying patient's repeated and considered desire for their sufferings to be brought to an end? In theory it is, certainly. But in everyday practice is there not a danger of adopting and proclaiming one attitude in order to avoid admitting to another?

The Committee of Ministers has observed on several occasions that the law in different countries treats the problem of euthanasia in a variety of ways. Recommendation 1418 has not succeeded in creating a single approach to this difficult, sensitive issue. As we have already observed, the Netherlands and Belgium have recently made new arrangements which diverge significantly from the principles set forth by the Assembly. There is undoubtedly an even wider discrepancy between the Parliamentary Assembly's position, with which the Committee of Ministers concurs, and the actual state of affairs: all the research shows that doctors and above all health care staff are regularly confronted with the problem of euthanasia.[1] They are usually left to deal unaided with the pleas for help they receive, and clarity and openness in the matter are distressingly absent. Recommendation 1418 set out the position as interpreted by the Parliamentary Assembly but seems not to have made much impact on the real world. This, clearly, is what led Belgian Senator Philippe Monfils to ask for the question to be re-examined:

"... the trend initiated by the new legislation in the Netherlands challenges the member states of the Council of Europe to examine the important social issue of euthanasia in the light of those moral and spiritual values in the organisation's Statute".[2]

We believe there are plenty of reasons for further Parliamentary Assembly debate, even if the eventual outcome is a restatement of the principles already laid down. It is impossible to ignore the new legislation in the Netherlands and Belgium or fail to acknowledge the long and serious debate which has taken place in those countries, which have a strong tradition of humanism. New legislation by two member states which in significant areas clearly diverges from Recommendation 1418 should be a matter of concern for both the Assembly and the Committee of Ministers. There is bound to be widespread interest in the initial results of this important change in legislative strategy. For example, it would be worth looking into the reasons for the drop in euthanasia cases in the Netherlands in each of the last two years.[1] Debate is also taking place in other European countries. In Switzerland, for example, public debate about the suicide assistance given by associations[2] whose members include both Protestant and Catholic clergy has contributed to a better understanding of the question, resulting in more openness and greater vigilance.[3]

Recommendation 1418 established the supremacy of one vision over another. It did not endeavour to reconcile the different positions, by attempting, for instance, to assess cultural difference as the explanatory factor where positions are divergent yet, as they often do, invoke the same, or at least equivalent, values. The Assembly has given clear support to an absolute prohibition on killing, a core principle of the monotheistic religions (though those same religions have argued for exceptions to it such as the death penalty or the concept of the "just" war). Some Protestant Churches, on the other hand, have come out in favour of the decriminalisation, on specific conditions, of direct active euthanasia, expressly approving the Dutch model.[4] In France, after wide-ranging debate, the National Consultative Committee on Ethics (CCNE) has delivered an opinion recognising disregard of the prohibition on killing as ethically legitimate in exceptional cases.[5]

A review of Recommendation 1418 thus seems necessary, however arduous (to judge from preliminary discussions) it might prove. This is a sensitive issue which arouses emotions and generates heated controversy. The Dutch and Belgian developments have triggered widespread debate and calls for legal reform are on the increase. In one of the most recent cases 80 French Socialist MPs tabled a bill, which was made public on 15 May 2003, calling on Parliament to introduce the right to a death of one's own choosing, in line with the existing right to live life as one saw fit.[6] In some other countries there is continued rejection of a more open approach.[7] Many would rather avoid renewed debate and keep to the recommendation voted in 1999 – even those who agree that it is probably unfair to treat as murderers people who accede to a dying person's insistent and thoroughly considered request for their life to be

1.
See *Le Temps*, 30 April 2003, p. 30.

2.
On the problem of "assisted suicide" and the Council of Europe, see the study, as yet only a working document, presented to a meeting of the European branch of the World Health Organisation in Copenhagen on 2 December 2002 by the office of the Council of Europe Human Rights Commissioner (Fernando Mora and Cristina Palazzo, "Assisted Suicide & the Council of Europe").

3.
Two years ago the city of Zurich rescinded a rule that associations providing suicide assistance were not to have access to hospital facilities. The decision sparked off bitter controversy, but in a report on its effects the municipality said there had been only 8 cases of assisted suicide in 2001 and 2002 and emphasised that the wave of suicides that some had feared had not materialised (*Neue Zürcher Zeitung*, 6 March 2003).

4.
Eg the Italian Protestant Church (see P. Ricca, *Eutanasia, la legge olandese e commenti*, Editrice Claudiana, 2002).

5.
Fin de vie, arrêt de vie, euthanasie. Decision 63, 27 January 2000, in *Les Cahiers du Comité consultatif national d'éthique*, April 2000, pp. 3-33.

6.
See *Le Monde* newspaper, 17 May 2003.

7.
The Hungarian Constitutional Court, in a judgment dated 28 April 2003, rejected a 1993 complaint that opposing a terminally ill person's wish to die was contrary to human dignity. Whilst taking note of the recent Dutch and Belgian measures, the court unanimously upheld that the right to life took precedence over the right to dignity. It also questioned the constitutionality of a 1997 law which laid down very strict conditions for refusal by a patient of certain types of treatment (*Neue Zürcher Zeitung*, 30 April 2003).

brought to an end in order to curtail their sufferings. They take the view that decriminalisation in such cases is pointless, impracticable and even dangerous: pointless because the number of prosecutions is minute in relation to the number of cases; impracticable because of the difficulty of legislating on a situation which in any event is always exceptional, therefore better left to the doctors and the rules of medical ethics; and dangerous because decriminalisation here officially weakens the prohibition on killing and is a step down the slippery slope. Others seem to opt for a purely ethical solution:

> "To refrain from legislating, in the direction either of greater permissiveness or greater restrictiveness, is surely to accept that moral permission to transgress is a matter not for the law but for individual conscience, in all its fragility when faced with the insoluble"?[1]

Is a Council of Europe position on euthanasia possible? Perhaps not. But refusing to talk about it is certainly no solution.

1.
Denis Müller, "Quelques aspects religieux et éthiques de l'euthanasie active directe", in *Choisir*, October 2000, p. 22.

Council of Europe Parliamentary Assembly Hearing on Euthanasia (extracts)

Paris, National Assembly, 25 October 2002

A hearing of the Social, Health and Family Affairs Committee of the Parliamentary Assembly was held in Paris on the theme of euthanasia, in October 2002. On the agenda were:

- an introductory statement on the purpose of the hearing;
- Parliamentary Assembly Recommendation 1418 (1999) on protection of the human rights and dignity of the terminally ill and the dying, and Committee of Ministers' replies of 30 October 2000 and 26 March 2002;
- legislation and practice in Council of Europe member states;
- legislation in the Netherlands and the new legislation in Belgium: reasons for the choice and first experiences;
- the practice of euthanasia in Europe;
- euthanasia: is there a need for legislation?
- question and answer sessions.

The practice of euthanasia in Europe: is it a medical reality?

Professor Denys Pellerin, Member of the French National Consultative Committee on Ethics

Is the practice of euthanasia a medical reality? The French National Consultative Committee on Ethics examined this question in its report (No. 58) entitled "Enlightened consent and information for persons engaged in care or research".

In this document the committee came out in favour of dispassionate public discussion of the problem of end-of-life accompaniment. The subject was given extensive coverage in three reports:[1] I shall refer to report No. 63.

In the course of many hearings held by the Committee on Ethics, and even within the committee, it was clear that a certain confusion prevails when people talk about euthanasia.

1.
No. 59 on ageing, No. 63 entitled "End of life, ending life, euthanasia" and No. 65 entitled "Ethical reflection on neonatal resuscitation".

It is undeniable that today, in France and in the rest of the western world, scientific progress and the desire for comfort have encouraged the appearance of a new demand for a better death. This aspiration for a "good death", a "beautiful death", is particularly widespread today, when 70% of our population die in hospitals or care homes.

Dying is still a grim, harrowing ordeal, and all we can do is try to ease the pain and anguish. And yet, when we are in good health we still think that we are in control of life and death.

Certain acts and attitudes today command a broad consensus and deserve to be encouraged. Medicine must provide comfort, care and accompaniment when it can no longer provide treatment. These acts reflect an awareness that the autonomy and self-respect of persons who have reached the end of their lives should be respected, in spite of and even because of their extreme vulnerability. In France, the right to palliative care is guaranteed under the Act of 9 June 1999. In addition, pursuant to the 4 March 2002 Act on the Rights of Patients, Article L.110-5 of the Public Health Code stipulates that :

> "[E]veryone has the right to pain-alleviation treatment. Pain shall in all circumstances be anticipated, assessed, taken into account and treated. Health care professionals shall use all means at their disposal to ensure for everyone a dignified life until the moment of death."

"Extraordinary treatment" is defined as "unreasonable obsti-nacy", "a stubborn refusal to recognise that a person is doomed to die and is not curable". It is rejected by all religious, ethical and professional standard-setting authorities.

Let me quote some trenchant sentences from the report of the Committee on Ethics:

> "Refusal of extraordinary treatment may indeed hasten the moment of death; by definition it implies acceptance of the risk that death may result from treatment to alleviate pain and from treatment being withheld or scaled down.

> The combat against pain, whatever forms it takes and whatever its outcome, is not a crime but is a duty for all caregivers.

When combating suffering responsibly and effectively, a doctor does not seek to kill, but if death does occur, it will do so peacefully at the moment it has chosen.

Such an attitude may also embody a rejection of inhumane situations, for example, when the aim of treatment is disproportionate to the real situation, or if to continue with active treatment would entail suffering disproportionate to an objective which is anyway unachievable.

Halting cardio-pulmonary assistance simply implies recognition that such treatment is pointless and that death is imminent. Refraining from pointless acts may reflect a real respect for the individual.

We do not deny that, in these various cases, a medical decision not to carry out or prolong resuscitation or a decision to provide deep sedation may hasten the moment of death.

This is not a deliberate ending of life, but an admission that the ensuing death is the consequence of the patient's illness.

By voicing such strong opinions, the Committee on Ethics signalled its refusal to join in the semantic debate on "passive" euthanasia. Refusal of extraordinary treatment, acceptance of palliative care and accompaniment of patients are measures which seek to make the last moments of existence an integral part of life, namely to show respect for patients right up to the end. Following this course should enable people to remain in control of their own death. This is the patient's responsibility, whilst politicians are responsible for providing the necessary financial backing.

Palliative care and accompaniment should reduce the number of requests for euthanasia from people at the end of their life. I am not thinking here of their relatives and friends, who will doubtless continue to reason like healthy persons. It is not certain that end-of-life care will be adequate to solve the problem of euthanasia, but it will enable euthanasia to be seen as a last resort rather than a forbidden remedy.

There will always be borderline cases. As a rule, the medical staff provide care and the patient wants to live. But there may be cases in which the will to live is lacking and the patient wants to bring life to an end. In these situations, which are increasingly rare, the Committee on Ethics strongly advocates that decisions to perform euthanasia should not be taken alone in an arbitrary fashion but should be the outcome of collective research and thinking that commands the fullest possible consensus within a team that is committed to search for the least unacceptable option. Euthanasia is practised today in an inegalitarian and anarchic fashion. It is an offence to cause death, for whatever reason. Taking such a decision will never become an ordinary, everyday act. However, where the law is concerned, these observations should not lead to the decriminalisation of euthanasia, and there should be no amendment of current definitions of offences in the criminal code. The act of euthanasia should continue to be subject to the law, but it should be carefully scrutinised if reported by its authors, so that the fullest light is shed on the exceptional circumstances that led to a life being ended and on the conditions in which this was done. It is up to the courts to appraise the situation with the compassionate attitude they adopt when they deliver an opinion based on collective thinking.

Dr Agnes van der Heide – Department of Public Health, Erasmus University, Rotterdam, the Netherlands

I would like to give you some of the main results of a study we carried out with the Free University of Amsterdam. It has only recently become possible to base the debate on empirical studies. The first results concerning the year 1990 were published in 1991 and there was a follow-up study in 1995.

In 1990 euthanasia cases represented 1.7% of the sample and physician-assisted suicides represented 0.2%, while 18.8% of cases involved administration of high doses of opioids and decisions to withdraw treatment were made in 17.9% of cases. These figures sparked off heated debate.

In 1995, the percentage of euthanasia cases rose to 2.4%, while the figure for physician-assisted suicides remained stable at 0.2%. The figures for administration of opioids and withdrawal of treatment were 19.1% and 20.2% respectively.

Only 18% of cases were notified in 1990 and 41% in 1995.

The average age of patients was less than 80 years. In 80% of the cases, the patients were suffering from cancer. In 70% of cases the doctor was a general practitioner, and in 90% of the cases it was estimated that life was shortened by less than a month. Pain was rarely mentioned as patients' sole motive; the great majority of patients wished to avoid pointless suffering.

We also have some figures for Belgium and Australia. We are carrying out a third survey, and will publish the results in April 2003.

Professor Stein Husebø, MD, National Project on Palliative Care for the Elderly, Bergen, Norway, and University of Vienna

I am one of the founders of the European Association for Palliative Care. I do not think that development of this kind of care is possible without a far-reaching debate on euthanasia.

I do not agree with those who say that euthanasia is practised everywhere on the same scale as in the Netherlands. A survey in Norway five years ago revealed that there were only twenty-odd cases per year.

In Germany and Austria, patients are kept alive by intensive care. This may not necessarily be in accordance with their wishes, but they may not be told that they are dying.

I teach palliative care and bioethics and I have observed that some students believe that palliative care is illegal.

I am a doctor myself, but I do not trust doctors. They should not be given euthanasia as a weapon if they are not good at palliative care. Some 95% of patients ask us to help them to live, not to die.

If euthanasia were as widespread throughout Europe as it is in the Netherlands, there would be some 200 000 cases per year. The question is a simple one: how many abuses can we accept – 5, 50, 500? Or do we feel that one is too many? I have come across many cases where a slight change of painkiller also changed the patient's wishes. And I know that many doctors are completely ignorant about palliative care. Why give them this weapon?

At a conference in Vienna, the doctor who spoke before me told the meeting that he had said to his father who was dying of cancer: "I'm going to give you some medication that will help you to die when you cannot stand the pain any longer". In reply I told him that he could indeed have said to his father, "I am going to kill you", but alternatively he could have said, "Father, I love you, you mean more to me than anyone else in the world, I am going to be here with you every day, hold you in my arms and get you the best painkillers".

The problem is that the quality of palliative care is inadequate and that patients sometimes endure so much suffering that they lose their will to live. I have practised euthanasia in an extreme situation of this kind and I was not prosecuted because of the extenuating circumstances.

I really think that our countries ought to have unambiguous legislation so that doctors know what is authorised and what is not.

Questions, answers and discussion

Ms Karen Sanders, Registered General Nurse, Senior Lecturer in Nursing and Health Care Ethics, South Bank University, London

I am both a senior lecturer and a nurse with expertise in intensive care and oncology. For the last five years I have served on the Royal College of Nursing's Ethics Forum.

From my own experience and my contacts with the sick, with students and colleagues, I know that some patients ask for assistance to die because they consider their quality of life to be unacceptable, despite receiving the best available palliative care. Their symptoms such as pain, incontinence, vomiting, inability to perform activities of daily living are intolerable.

Sometimes, when patients ask for assistance to die, doctors prescribe increased doses of opioids, even when there is no imperative to do so on grounds of physical pain, doubtless with the intention of hastening their death. In that situation the health care team can hide behind the double effect rule. As for withholding or withdrawing treatment, leading to the patient's death, whether this is euthanasia or good health care practice depends on the intention of the health care team.

In the United Kingdom, the situation is similar to that in the Netherlands and in Belgium before they passed their assisted-dying legislation. Patients ask to be helped to die, and a significant number of health care professionals would like to comply, irrespective of the law.

Almost 60% of doctors questioned by the *British Medical Journal* some years ago said they had been asked to hasten death; 32% said they had complied with such a request; and 46% said they would consider helping someone to die if it were legal to do so. A later survey in the journal *Doctor* showed that 44% of the doctors questioned supported a change in the law to allow voluntary euthanasia, 35% had received requests from patients for active euthanasia, and 43% would consider practising voluntary euthanasia if it were legal. In a 1998 survey carried out by the *Sunday Times*, 14% of the doctors who answered admitted that they had helped a patient to die at their request. Some 38% of psychiatrists questioned by the *Lancet*, again in 1998, agreed that assisted suicide should be legal, whilst 44% disagreed. In a 1999 health care poll, medical practitioners were informed that physician-assisted suicide had been legal in the US State of Oregon since 1997 and were asked whether the law should be changed in the United Kingdom on similar lines; 28% answered yes and 65% no.

Fewer surveys of nurses have been carried out, but their results tend to be similar. In 1995, 23% of nurses questioned by the *Nursing Times* said that they had been requested by a member of medical staff to participate in performing euthanasia. Some 14% believed that requests for active euthanasia should be granted always, 54% sometimes and 32% never.

It can be seen that British law does not reflect what appears to be happening in the UK. This is why the Ethics Forum should ask the government to undertake detailed research into this matter.

Ms Joyce Robins, Co-Director, Patient Concern, London

I have no medical training, but I have personally experienced situations on two occasions, forty years ago and six months ago, in which euthanasia was practised.

In many cases, unfortunately, British law is so constituted that things are hushed up and friends and relatives are not even kept informed so that they can say farewell to someone who is going to die. In point of fact, secrecy offers no protection.

It is said that when the possibility of euthanasia is available, there are risks of abuse. But the risks are far greater at present: patients are involved in a lottery; they may come across a doctor who is willing to administer a lethal dose or they may be treated by another who is unwilling to do so through fear of prosecution. We have not made much progress, really, in the last forty years.

Patient Concern is not a pro-euthanasia organisation. We simply want the patient's choice to be accepted. The end of life is a time when it is important for this choice to be exercised. However, in the hospital environment, where most of us will die, this choice is in the doctors' hands.

The messages we receive from patients are contradictory. Many talk of long-term suffering leading to a miserable death. Others talk of doctors secretly hastening death on compassionate grounds. Many believe that their relatives died too soon because doctors administered large doses of drugs or withdrew treatment without consultation. Clearly it is a lottery, depending on the individual position of the doctor.

Doctors have decided that it is ethical and the courts have held it as lawful to withdraw treatment, causing patients to die slowly – yet we are told that it is both unethical and unlawful to give patients dying in misery a simple injection to give them a quick end. I hear all the arguments about omission as opposed to commission but to the patients on the receiving end, it may seem a strange argument.

We have to be open-minded and no longer hide behind the mantra "there can never be any legal justification for actions intended to bring about death". Nor can we believe that palliative care can take away all the horrors. We cannot go on pretending that because the law against euthanasia is there for most of us, all is well and that any change will put patients in fear. Patients are frightened about what is going on now. We must face the facts, evaluate them and set up a realistic framework which will allow patients to make their choice.

Dr Jean-Marie Gomas, Pain and Palliative Care Centre, Sainte Perine Hospital, Paris

I am a general practitioner, a hospital doctor and a clinician.

Euthanasia has existed since time immemorial, since we have been confronted with meaninglessness and despair. What is more, we live in a society which is obsessed with control, regulation, the courts – a society which wants to control everything. It is time to say that this is just not possible.

In the course of the proceedings, I have been struck by the caricatured, stereotyped and violent nature of certain expressions such as "pitiful", "decline", "crime", "pull the trigger", etc. Individually, everyone is free to think what they want about life, death, suicide and the reasons why, for them, life is not worth living. But collective clinical wisdom must qualify these individual positions, which are unacceptable in terms of their violence and the moral judgment they imply.

Furthermore, contrary to what has been said at least twenty times since this morning, dignity is not only physical, it is not only in the body, but is rooted in interpersonal relationships, in our interaction with others. Otherwise some of us might already have no dignity left. There is no such thing as a "dignity meter".

I have been struck by the "certainness" of some statements, whereas the patient lives in ambivalence: he knows he is going to die, but cannot believe it; how would he know what he really wants? Who can pride himself on always understanding the wishes of others? We ourselves are all convinced that we are going to control our own destiny, but we do not have the answer to everything. So let us not lead users of the health system to believe that we do, because there will always be situations which cannot be controlled: tragedy is unavoidable.

I also heard the words "abuses", "aberrations" and "scandalous". Yes, it is scandalous to shorten the life of a patient who has not asked to die, and yet that does happen, right here in Paris. But the subject of today's discussion is shortening the life of a patient who has asked to die. We are told that active euthanasia is often requested by patients, the family and the doctor in order not to end up "like a vegetable", to preserve their dignity, to put an end to dreadful suffering, because life no longer has any meaning. But this is the crux of the matter: there are tetraplegics for whom life still has a meaning, who do not ask for euthanasia, and there are people who are still walking who do ask for euthanasia. How could a single rule be found?

The word "unbearable" has been used a great deal. But for whom is the suffering "unbearable"? If it is the patient, he alone has the right to say so. But "unbearableness" can also be seen in the eyes of others, and that brings us back to the virtual mirage of a "dignity meter", which cannot exist.

When it comes to relieving the suffering of a patient in the terminal stages of an illness who has asked for euthanasia, each case is different. But decisions by the politicians in charge of the health system tend to stress the human being inside the patient. Patients want respect for their rights, and they are right.

On a daily basis I cannot find a solution to everything. In most cases, patients feel that their suffering is recognised and do not ask for euthanasia. Those who do so have no other solution, but I do not think that legislation is the right answer. It is too early and too risky. We must continue to fight for respect for the patient.

Ms Patrizia Paoletti-Tangheroni, member of the Social, Health and Family Affairs Committee of the Parliamentary Assembly, Italy

This issue should not be approached superficially or hastily. Of course we have to make choices but in a context of objectives and values that we share, as specialists and politicians. The broadest possible consensus must be sought.

It is sometimes thought that euthanasia is a better solution than withdrawing treatment, which is something quite different.

We must press on with research into the fight against pain and avoid giving different treatment to rich and poor.

Some people maintain that we are sometimes afraid to admit the existence of euthanasia. The problem does not arise in these terms. We only talk about "euthanasia" where there is a law. Everywhere else all we see are deaths and suicides.

And are the doctors ready? Not where I come from.

There are some very moving stories about people who have chosen to die, but most people want to go on living. Let us think about a Nobel Peace laureate who strove to give a good death to those who had lost all dignity: Mother Teresa.

Dr Philippe Maassen, member of the Euthanasia Law Monitoring Committee, Belgium

I am a general practitioner and I do not work in a hospital environment.

End-of-life accompaniment is an exceptional act. In my view, it is not a moment in time but a journey. A doctor's mission is to prolong the life entrusted to him or her by a patient. When pathology makes an end-of-life act necessary, the latter results from a contract between the doctor and a patient he or she has known for a long time. That is very different from what happens in hospital.

In Belgium, what has been changed by the euthanasia debate is that patients feel empowered to talk about the subject. Confidence is the most important thing. This morning, one of our specialists said that patients may be afraid of being killed by their doctor. When people want to know, they are not afraid of giving their trust. What patients fear most is not suffering but pointless suffering.

To those who fear that euthanasia might be forced on them I would say that nothing is worse than letting things happen in silence and in secrecy.

Mr Claude Evin, Member of the Social, Health and Family Affairs Committee of the Parliamentary Assembly, France

Where health is concerned, the legislator should act with considerable modesty.

We all agree that patients should not suffer pointlessly. Patients must be listened to. As a legislator, I wonder whether the right answer is to make it legal for one person to cause another's death. Thanks to Mr Monfils [Mr Philippe Monfils, Senator, Belgium, member of the committee], I have been able to study the Belgian law, which is very interesting. But I still have some queries. Can a society authorise a person to procure another person's death? Are there no other solutions? In France, the Act of 4 March 2002 defines the rights of patients and recognises the autonomy of the human person. I was rapporteur of this text and I heard statements from many health professionals. Like Mr Gomas, I think it is too early to legislate, although I realise that in some situations health professionals are short of tools. Until we have made sure that patients' rights are respected, I do not see how we can contemplate allowing someone to legally cause death.

The health care professions are still very reluctant to accept the principle of the patient's autonomy. This is why patients are sometimes afraid that the doctor will take decisions for them.

Like Mr Neuwirth [Mr Lucien Neuwirth, Honorary Member of the Parliamentary Assembly, France], I think the first thing to do is manage pain. We should not let it be thought that deciding to cause death is like waving a magic wand. The law will never be able to provide all the answers, although the Belgian and Netherlands laws are extremely interesting. First of all, we must fight for respect for the rights of the person and the Council of Europe can make a contribution to this.

Patients have their rights, including the right to be heard and the right to consent.

Professor John Keown, Rose F. Kennedy Chair in Christian Ethics, Georgetown University, Washington DC

Contrary to what Dr van der Heide said, there have been thousands of cases of euthanasia in the Netherlands where the patient has not requested it.

Ms Sanders, it is possible to help someone to die without intentionally causing their death. What do you want to do in Britain? If euthanasia is not controlled in the Netherlands, why would it be elsewhere?

Ms Jacqueline Herremans, President of the Association for the Right to Die in Dignity, Brussels, and member of the Commission for the Supervision and Evaluation of the Law on Euthanasia

In reply to Mr Evin, I would like to point out that under the Dutch Civil Code patients must give their consent. In Belgium we have just passed a law on patients' rights. We did not only consider the problem of euthanasia, but that of doctor-patient relationships in general. I cannot therefore accept the argument that we are not ready.

Mr Husebø does not have confidence in his colleagues. I must be more trusting than he is. At all events, I have noticed that responsibility for the decision has shifted: in the past, doctors were all powerful, but now the trend is towards a close dialogue between patient and doctor. Is this the right time to lose confidence in doctors?

I am amazed at the humility shown by some people who consider that we are not ready. On the contrary, we must press ahead and place our faith in humankind.

Dr Agnes van der Heide

Mr Keown, out of a thousand cases in which a doctor caused death without an explicit request from the patient, in half of them it is known that the patient had asked for assistance to die in the past. The other 500 cases are extremely heterogeneous in nature, some patients being in such a condition that they could no longer take a decision. I do not deny that there may be some problematic cases: this must be discussed.

Turning to explicit requests, 74% of them are motivated by unbearable suffering, 56% wish to avoid an undignified death, 47% want to prevent worse suffering and 30% feel they are suffering pointlessly.

Ms Karen Sanders

The question is less one of knowing how many sick people ask for euthanasia than of knowing whether or not it is voluntary. From this point of view it would be interesting to know what is really happening in the United Kingdom.

Ms Joyce Robins

I do not want more patients to be killed, I want more to be saved. Of course, there will still be abuses if we change the law, but patients will then have a real choice and we shall know what is actually happening, because it is really dangerous not to know.

If palliative care did all that some speakers claim for it, then no patients would be asking for euthanasia. In the Netherlands many patients explore the possibilities of euthanasia but very few go through with it. Many people learn to live with the disease that afflicts them and with what happens to them. But it is those who do not manage to do so that we are talking about here. I repeat, it is a question of choice for the patients.

Dr Stein Husebø

It is important to agree on definitions. If the doctors do not know the difference between passive and active euthanasia how can public opinion know?

It is very difficult to kill a patient. A little more – even five times more – morphine would not do it. You have to know the active principle.

If you feel that your life and your suffering are unbearable and society suggests that you bring them to an end, does that not create a demand?

Professor Denys Pellerin

I should like to come back to the persistent confusion between passive and active euthanasia.

At the terminal stage, where therapeutic measures are no longer appropriate, it is essential that patients are not only accompanied but given appropriate assistance to reduce their suffering, even if this means shortening the few hours of life remaining to them.

However, the National Consultative Committee on Ethics acknowledges that severe chronic conditions also exist which render everyday life unbearable. We are all aware of heart-breaking examples, especially concerning certain neurological diseases that are not only irreversible but, even worse, progressive.

However, such situations do not necessarily call for legislation. It should be possible to provide individual responses, where the wishes of the individual concerned have been known for a long time, and reiterated until the last time their wishes were expressed; if the decision is neither clandestine nor hypocritical, but reached in a mature way by those facing their last moments, in an atmosphere of shared trust with their loved ones and care team.

Here, I should like to note that these conclusions by the Consultative Committee on Ethics have given rise to inaccurate interpretations.

Headlines such as "The Consultative Committee on Ethics allows euthanasia in exceptional circumstances" have appeared. The committee was then asked to draw up a list of these exceptions. A deliberate misrepresentation of information? – or, more probably, a failure in communication, since the committee had clearly stated that, without there being any need to decriminalise the offence, it was possible to explain to a judge the reasons and circumstances behind particular decisions and acts. There would have to be due compliance with certain conditions for the conduct in question to be acceptable, in the name of solidarity and respect for personal dignity.

Article 346 of the French Code of Criminal Procedure in fact provides for exceptional situations. It was for this reason that the committee considered that proceedings could be dismissed in situations where those responsible would normally be charged.

Finally, I should like to come back to a comment by Mr Claude Evin on patients' rights, and clarify it. All too often, information from a patient's file is communicated poorly in hospitals, particularly in emergency services. Acutely ill patients admitted to emergency units are still too often dealt with as though they were new cases, rather than patients with an existing medical file. Yet this file can – indeed, should – indicate whether the person concerned has refused a particular treatment in the event of a relapse. This is a difficult problem to solve, since it is linked to the organisation of our health care system. We must improve the way in which people's wishes are set down in their medical file, so that these wishes are scrupulously respected in all circumstances, even and perhaps especially when the person is not in a fit state to be questioned.

Dr Gomas

It must be realised that wishes, whatever they may be, change constantly. Moreover, palliative care does not do away with the request for euthanasia, as that stems from hopelessness and fear of death. The most difficult patients to treat are not necessarily cancer patients in the terminal stages, but the chronically disabled faced with hopelessness, in some cases for over thirty years. We still have a great deal of work to do here.

The law and practices of Council of Europe member states concerning euthanasia

by Elaine Gadd

Do you think euthanasia should be allowed? It is tempting to answer "yes" or "no", but a Council of Europe survey has shown the importance of first asking "What do you mean by 'euthanasia'?". Only a few states have defined the term legally, and in everyday language the practices covered by the term may range from a deliberate action to kill a person to withdrawing life sustaining medical treatment. The Parliamentary Assembly issued a recommendation in 1999 on the protection of the human rights and dignity of the terminally ill and dying, which highlighted the importance of medical decision-making at the end of life.[1]

To obtain an overview of the present situation in Europe, in 2001-02, the Council of Europe's Steering Committee on Bioethics conducted a questionnaire survey of the member states concerning their laws and practices with regard to euthanasia and certain other issues relevant to decision-making at the end of life at the request of the Committee of Ministers. The survey aimed to clarify how states described and applied different concepts, such as active and passive euthanasia, assisted suicide and withdrawal of treatment. Variations in approach depending on the person's situation – for example, if the person was or was not able to consent, or was brain dead – were also explored. Thirty-four states responded,[2] and this chapter describes some of the results.

Although terms such as "euthanasia", "active euthanasia" and "passive euthanasia" were generally recognised, few states used such terms in legislation. If the terms were legally defined, their scope varied widely, for example from the Russian Federation which legally defines euthanasia as "complying with the request of a patient to hasten his (her) death with some action or means, including discontinuing of life sustaining treatment" to the Netherlands which defines it as "termination of life by a doctor at the voluntary and carefully

1.
Recommendation 1418 (1999).

2.
Full details of the responses are available at www.coe.int/bioethics

considered request of a patient". Generally, the term "active euthanasia" is used to describe carrying out a procedure intended to lead to the patient's death, and "passive euthanasia" the situation when medical treatment is withdrawn or withheld and the patient dies of the condition from which he or she was suffering.

In Belgium and the Netherlands, it is now legally permissible for a physician to terminate life if certain conditions are met. In both countries, the patient must make a voluntary, carefully considered and repeated request, and must have been informed about his or her health situation and what the future is likely to hold in this respect. The patient must be suffering unbearably without prospect of improvement, and there must be (in the view of both physician and patient) no reasonable alternative to euthanasia. A second independent physician must also see the patient. In both countries, it is possible for patients who know that later in the development of their illness (for example, because they will become unconscious) they will not be able to make the request to make it in advance to be acted on at a later stage. In both countries there are additional specific procedural requirements that must be complied with, including arrangements to ensure that use of euthanasia can be monitored.

In both Belgium and the Netherlands it is unlawful for anyone except a physician to perform euthanasia, and in the other European states it is unlawful for anyone to deliberately terminate the life of another, for example by giving a poison. In many states, this is regulated by the law on homicide or murder. However, some states consider that killing someone at that person's own request is rather different from homicide in other circumstances. For example, the punishment for homicide in Portugal is between eight and fifteen years' imprisonment, but homicide at the request of the victim is punished by a lesser sentence, of between one and five years in prison. In Greece, if homicide were to be carried out for merciful reasons on a person suffering from an incurable disease, at his or her serious and persistent request, the sentence can be as short as ten days in prison.

In most Council of Europe member states, it is also unlawful to assist a person to commit suicide. In Estonia, the Netherlands and Switzerland it may be permissible in certain circumstances; for example, in Switzerland it will not be a crime if the person who assists is not driven by a selfish motive. In some countries, as with the laws on homicide, if assisting suicide is unlawful the penalties may be reduced in some situations. For example, in Norway the penalty will be more lenient if a person, motivated by compassion, has assisted in the killing of a terminally ill person. In some countries, such as Luxembourg, where suicide is not a crime, assisting suicide is also not considered a crime in itself, but a person may still be subject to penalties for the "non-assistance of a person in danger".

In contrast, in most states it is lawful to withhold or withdraw life-prolonging medical treatment in certain circumstances. All the states who responded to the questionnaire said that if a person were able to give or refuse to give consent, and were to refuse a specific treatment, this refusal must be respected by health care staff. However, there are a few exceptions in specific situations. For example, in Georgia a pregnant woman does not have the right to refuse a medical intervention which is necessary for the birth of a live foetus if it poses only a minimal risk to her own life and health. Children may also not have the same rights to refuse treatment as do adults in the same country.

The procedures that are required for a person to be diagnosed as "brain dead" vary slightly from country to country. In some countries, such as Slovenia, the criteria are set out in a law, whereas in other countries, such as Italy, the criteria are set out in a professional code of practice. The extent to which countries require particular types of radiological tests varies. However, in every country apart from the Russian Federation, once a patient has been declared brain dead according to the criteria in force, it is lawful to withdraw any medical intervention that the person is receiving, as treatment can no longer benefit the person.

However, while there seems to be widespread agreement that it is ethically acceptable to withdraw treatment at an adult patient's request, or if a person is brain dead, there is more controversy about whether it is acceptable to withdraw life-prolonging treatment from a person who is not able to consent (or to refuse) treatment, for example because they were in a coma.

Some countries have made provision for advance directives, which are sometimes called "living wills". An advance directive is made by a person able to consent who, in the same way that we decide in an ordinary will what we would like to happen to our possessions after we die, decides what medical treatment they would like if they were not able to express a choice at the time the treatment was needed. Obviously, none of us can know exactly what treatment we might need in the future. However, if people know that they have a particular illness (such as dementia or multiple sclerosis) that will get worse in the future, and which may mean that they will no longer be able to take decisions personally, they can discuss with their physician what is likely to happen and so form a view of how they would like to be treated at particular stages of the illness.

Article 9 of the Convention on Human Rights and Biomedicine sets out the rule that a person's previously expressed wishes about a medical intervention (which could be set out in an advance directive) should be taken into account when deciding whether or not a person unable to consent should be given that intervention. However, there is a difference between something being taken into account, and it being legally binding. About a quarter of Council of Europe states have provisions that make advance directives legally binding in some circumstances – which means they have to be respected even if the physician, or the person's family, disagrees with the request. However, physicians cannot be made to provide treatment that is illegal (such as euthanasia in states where it is not lawful), nor treatment that is inappropriate for the person's condition. So in practice, legally binding advance directives usually apply to refusals of particular types of treatment.

In some countries, such as Hungary, for an advance directive to be valid the law requires it to be made in a particular form. Other countries, for example Slovenia and Spain, require that it be witnessed. In Denmark, living wills are registered at the Danish Living Will Register, so that if a patient has lost the capacity to take decisions personally, the physician can consult the Data Register before starting (or in some circumstances, continuing) life-prolonging treatment to ensure that any treatment would accord with the patient's wishes.

In countries, such as Germany or Finland, where advance directives have the potential to be legally binding, there may be exceptions if the directive is old, particularly if new treatments have become available for the patient's condition, as it may not be clear that the directive really reflects what the patient would now want. In France, where advance directives are not legally binding, the law allows a person able to consent to nominate a "person of confidence" who must be consulted by the health care team if the patient is not able to take decisions him or herself. Other states, such as Norway, have procedures that mean that the patient's next of kin is consulted in such circumstances. This is another way for a patient to ensure that the treatment they receive is what they would want. In the United States of America, some states allow patients to nominate another person to take legally binding decisions on medical treatment on their behalf if they cannot take those decisions personally.

If a country does not have provisions that allow the use of advance directives or a person of confidence, this does not mean that life-prolonging treatment has to be continued in all circumstances when a person is not able to take decisions personally. This reflects a recognition that what is sometimes called "therapeutic relentlessness" may not be in the interests of the patient, and that if a treatment is futile, or causing more suffering than benefit, it may not be right to continue it. The majority of the Council of Europe states allow life-prolonging treatment to be withdrawn from a person not able to consent in some circumstances, although this is not permitted in countries such as Estonia, Greece, the Russian Federation and Sweden.

In conclusion, it is unlawful in the majority of Council of Europe states to carry out either active euthanasia or to assist a person to commit suicide. Whether such activities should be lawful is actively debated by both the public and by professional and other groups, with strong views on both sides of the argument. In contrast, there is more variation between states on attitudes to other aspects of end-of-life decision-making, such as withdrawing and withholding treatment or the extent to which advance directives are considered to be legally binding. Advances in medical treatment mean that there are now increasing possibilities for keeping people alive in situations when death would previously have been inevitable. However, the burdens that such treatments may impose, and whether or not it is good to be kept alive in certain conditions – for example, if the person is no longer able to communicate or interact with others or take any form of independent action – is a matter on which many people have strong views, which will ensure that end-of-life decision-making will be actively debated for years to come.

The need for more palliative care

by Piotr Mierzewski

In ageing European societies a 20% increase in the need for palliative care is to be expected, both for cancer and for non-cancer patients in the next ten to fifteen years. This poses great challenges, both quantitative and qualitative, for all European countries: it requires the development of coherent policies on palliative care, integrated into existing health care systems. It raises the important political question of to what extent societies feel responsible for the quality of the last phase of their citizens' lives.

The time is ripe

The modern history of palliative care began in 1967, when Dame Cicely Saunders founded St Christopher's Hospice in London, a pioneer in this area. Since then palliative care has spread all over Europe, despite the challenges, which include scarce resources, poor availability of medical drugs and lack of understanding among the public and health professionals. The idea of palliative care may be new to many people, but it is perhaps one of the oldest medical specialities – the care of the vulnerable was a primary task of medieval hospices, when treatment was not available. The evidence base has grown and good practice models have been developed – the time has come to consolidate the best experience available in Europe.

European Health Committee (CDSP): bridging principles and practice

One of the goals of the Council of Europe is to assist member states to create a harmonious "ethical framework" for their health systems, promoting the same ethical and human rights principles across the entire continent.

The value framework and legal provisions have to be translated into practical policy developments. The CDSP, supported by a secretariat – the Health Division in Directorate General III (Social Cohesion) – undertakes this work.

The role of the CDSP is to prepare practical guidelines on health policy in the form of recommendations for adoption by the Committee of Ministers, the Council's executive body. These recommendations are non-binding in a legal sense, but as a sign of consensus and political commitment they have the advantage of influencing health policies without subjecting implementation to precise conditions and time-limits. They are often used by professionals and non-governmental organisations as vehicles for advocating change.

For years the recommendations, within the health sector, dealt with different categories of vulnerable populations: prisoners, the elderly, the chronically ill and the socially excluded. People towards the end of their life are particularly vulnerable and in need of special protection. This recognition led to a recommendation on the organisation of palliative care, drafted by an expert committee after two years' work, which was adopted by the Committee of Ministers in November 2003.[1] The committee was chaired by Tony O'Brien who gave an overview of the issue in the first volume of this book. The work of the expert committee was supported by representatives from the WHO, the European Association of Palliative Care and the Palliative Care in Eastern Europe (EAPC) Project.

The selection of palliative care as an important topic was also inspired by Parliamentary Assembly Recommendation 1418 (1999) on the protection of the human rights and dignity of the terminally ill and the dying, by earlier Assembly texts (Resolution 613 (1976) and Recommendation 779 (1976)) and by the 1980 report of the CDSP on "Problems related to death: care for the dying". These documents called for integrated support for patients and their families and comprehensive management of their suffering.

Holistic scope of the recommendation

The task of the committee was to prepare a recommendation on the basis of the current state of the art of palliative care in member countries, and in particular on:

– the legislative framework needed for the development of palliative care;

1.
Recommendation
Rec (2003)24 of the
Council of Europe's
Committee of Ministers, see Appendix VI.

- the development of structures for the practice of palliative care in the widest sense and for the wide family circle;
- the reform of medical practice with regard to terminally ill persons, and particularly in cases of excessively prolonged treatment;
- innovative approaches such as palliative day care and home care;
- improving training for health professionals on their role in the proper use of palliative care.

One should remember that in Latin the word "patient" meant both a sufferer and somebody with a lot of patience. Nowadays, everybody becomes a patient one day. The journey of life is intertwined with a journey of care from birth to death, we rely on health care institutions. For many, the final station of the journey of life is that of the journey of care – in palliative care institutions. The approach to palliative care should therefore be based on a global vision of therapeutic activity, not limited to symptom control but focusing on the continuity of care until death.

Past, present, and future challenges

Past challenges	Present challenges	Future challenges
• Establishing a service • Building a scientific foundation for palliative care • Integrating hospices into the mainstream health care system • Putting emphasis on cancer patients	• Building institutional infrastructure • Obtaining secure financing • Building a solid base of evidence with proven research findings • Teaching and training new professionals	• Extending care to patients nearing the end of life with non-malignant conditions • Promoting palliative care Europe-wide • Creating a positive image of palliative care

The integrated approach – Cure, care, communication, companionship and compassion brought together

These five "C" words put in a nutshell the vocation of modern palliative care. Although it cannot add days to the patient's life, it certainly adds life to the patient's days.

The recommendation declares in the preamble that:

– palliative care is the active, total care of patients with advanced, progressive diseases, aiming at the control of pain and other symptoms, and offering psychological, social and spiritual support;

– the goal of palliative care is the achievement of the best possible quality of life for patients and their families;

– palliative care aims to help men, women and children with advanced, progressive diseases to enjoy the best possible quality of life until the end, and intends neither to hasten nor postpone death;

– palliative care affirms life and regards dying as a normal process, and is not guided by hopelessness or fatalism;

– all people near the end of life desire to be treated as valued persons by health care professionals and to have skilled attention directed at maintaining dignity and fostering independence, relieving symptoms and maximising comfort;

– palliative care, like all medical care, should be patient-oriented, guided by the needs of the patient, taking into account his or her values and preferences, and that dignity and autonomy are central issues for patients in need of palliative care;

– the differences in the availability and quality of palliative care throughout Europe need to be addressed through increased co-operation between countries;

– palliative care is an integral part of the health care system and an inalienable element of a citizen's right to health care, and that therefore it is a responsibility of the government to guarantee that palliative care is available to all who need it.

The Committee of Ministers therefore recommends that the governments of member states adopt policies, legislative and other measures necessary for a coherent and comprehensive national policy framework for palliative care.

Core elements of a national policy framework for palliative care

Guiding principles

The well-known value framework of the Council of Europe helped to develop the principles underpinning the recommendation, many of which were mentioned previously as part of the preamble (integration, quality of life, patient-oriented). Other important ones are:

- incorporation into national health strategies;
- equity in access according to needs, without undue delay, in a setting which is consistent with patients' needs and preferences;
- addressing physical, psychological and spiritual issues associated with advanced disease;
- the right to treatment of intervening problems if the patient so wishes, linked with the right to refuse it, while receiving the best palliative care, if the patient prefers;
- an adequate and equitable level of funding.

It is clear from the above that palliative care does not address a specific disease and spans the period from the diagnosis of advanced disease until the end of bereavement and is not identical with terminal care, but encompasses it. Palliative care affirms life and regards dying as a normal process. Patients' death is not seen as a professional failure – professionals should recognise the limits of medicine and refrain from over treatment.

Relationship to euthanasia

It important to note that euthanasia and physician-assisted suicide are not included in any definition of palliative care; for that reason, the recommendation does not take a stand on these issues. Palliative care intends neither to hasten nor postpone death. Palliative care interventions are not and should not be designed to end life prematurely. Equally, it is important that the technologies available in modern medical practice are not applied to prolonging life unnaturally. Doctors are not obliged to continue forms of treatment that are patently futile and excessively burdensome to the patient. Equally, patients are entitled to refuse medical treatment. In palliative care, the objective is to ensure that patients have the highest possible quality of life. At the point when the disease process is bringing that life to a natural end, patients must be able to receive every possible measure of physical, emotional and spiritual comfort.

Settings and services

The emphasis is on:

- the interdisciplinarity (a whole team's responsibility) and multiprofessonality (hierarchy retained) approaches to palliative care;

- a wide range of resources, such as home care, in-patient care in specific or conventional units, day hospitals and out-patient clinics, emergency call-out, and respite care facilities;

- support for informal caregivers;

- availability of specialist palliative care for all patients when they need it, at any time and in any situation;

- availability of sufficient respite care facilities to offer temporary relief for caregivers.

By far the largest proportion of palliative care is given in the home and by non-specialist services. Specialised services are fully devoted to palliative care, whose teams are specially trained in this area of care. Such services do not take the place of care provided by front-line professionals, but support and complement such care according to the needs identified and the complexity of the situation. A rough estimate of the need of palliative care beds is 50-100 per million inhabitants.

Policy and organisation

Policy development should start with a needs assessment study, leading to palliative care strategies. Legal, social, economic, cultural, administrative and/or physical barriers in access to palliative care services should be identified

The availability of narcotic drugs is a specific concern since their availability is often insufficient owing to legal restrictions, both in terms of the variety of opioids available and different dose regimens. It is proposed that legislation should make opioids and other drugs accessible in a range of formulations and dosages for medical use. The fear of abuse should not hinder access to necessary and effective medication.

Special attention should be paid to palliative care for under-privileged groups and to cultural and ethnic differences related to the needs of patients. Equally importantly, special attention should be paid to palliative care for children.

Authorities are encouraged to publish a national annual report on the organisation and functioning of palliative care.

Quality improvement and research

In general, quality improvement in palliative care is no different from quality improvement in health care as described in Council of Europe Parliamentary Assembly Recommendation (97) 17. However, there are some specific dimensions of palliative care (the overriding importance of patient preferences, the family as the unit of care, the importance of spiritual and existential issues, and the involvement of non-professionals).

There is still a need to develop indicators of good palliative care and performance, and clinical practice guidelines developed with the participation of patients, leading to a coherent national monitoring strategy.

Recognising gaps in the base of evidence, the recommendation calls for collaborative research, both at national and at European level, and advises governments to establish an observatory to collect, process and disseminate reliable information on developments in and the quality of palliative care.

Education and training

Education of professionals and of the public is regarded as the key to the development of palliative care everywhere. In all countries there should be three levels of (continuing) education for professionals: basic, intermediary and advanced. Some countries recognise specialisation in palliative care.

The greatest emphasis should be on communication skills (breaking bad news), changing the unjustified negative images concerning opioids and devoting attention to spiritual and cultural aspects.

Special attention should be given to educating the general public, in order to change the negative, fatalistic image of palliative care.

The family

The family is defined in broad terms as those close to patients. It needs assistance and support in developing the ability to give emotional and practical support to patients, to adapt to the process, and to cope with grief and loss.

Communicating with patient and family

This is a cornerstone of palliative care. Openness, the exchange of information, mutual understanding, support and commitment, addressing difficult and sometimes painful issues and dealing with emotional distress, and a genuine wish to hear and understand the concerns of another are the guiding principles.

A special issue is the extent to which patients wish to be informed about their situation; in this regard, attention should be paid to cultural differences and the wishes of patients. Providing information at sufficiently wide intervals and giving patients and families the time to take in the bad news has proved to be essential.

Where there are no good answers, it is important to stay with the person and try to empathise with their sufferings.

Teams, teamwork and care planning

Palliative care by its very nature is an interdisciplinary and multiprofessional undertaking, which should be shared between the patient, the family and the team, whenever this is appropriate and would comply fully with the patients' wishes.

Volunteers play a special role, not taking over the work of professionals, but bringing their own contribution and expertise. Governments are requested to facilitate the setting-up of volunteer services. To be credible partners, voluntary helpers must be trained, closely monitored and approved by an association. Training is essential and must be preceded by careful selection. Willingness to help is not enough. In an age when the subject of death is taboo, the presence of voluntary helpers alongside professional caregivers also has an important symbolic value. They "resocialise" death and show that it is not only a matter for health professionals, but also a problem for society as a whole.

Voluntary helpers form a team working under the responsibility of a co-ordinator, who serves as a link between the voluntary helpers and the carers, and between the hospital and the association.

The recommendation makes a distinction between interdisciplinary and multidisciplinary teams. Leadership of the interdisciplinary team is dependent on the task at hand, not on professional hierarchy, as is the case with multidisciplinary teams. It is required that at least the lead person in each professional group should be a trained and acknowledged specialist in palliative care.

A leading co-ordinator, preferably the primary physician, should guarantee the coherence of messages from different care providers. All communication between professionals concerning patients and families is subject to professional secrecy, fully respecting the patient's right to medical secrecy and the families' right to privacy.

Palliative care is usually very rewarding, but caring for the caregivers is needed to avoid a "burnout" syndrome.

Care planning and advance directives

Care planning and advance directives are not within the remit of the expert committee and are not tackled in the recommendation. However, being closely related to palliative care, they are discussed in the explanatory memorandum.

Even though the ethical assessment of decisions during the final period of a person's life varies among physicians, there is a common view that professional caregivers need to be capable of open discussion with their patients.

Ethical dilemmas may notably occur when a patient persistently wishes to die, even if there are further palliative options available. Depending on the extent to which patients bring up the issue, physicians should be prepared to explain their views on physician-assisted death (assisted suicide and euthanasia).

Bereavement

The recommendation recognises that bereavement support is regarded as an essential part of palliative care programmes, a view not shared by all. The rationale is that bereavement usually starts before the actual demise of the patient, because the palliative phase of disease is essentially a period of increasing loss, both to the patient and the family. Moreover, the family (not necessarily consisting of blood relatives) is regarded as the "unit of care". This makes it logical to continue, as far as necessary, the caring relationship with the family after the death of the patient.

Preparation for loss is already part of the grieving process. Bereavement support can therefore be provided before, during and after the loved one's death.

Cure, care, communication, companionship and compassion brought together

The Council of Europe's recommendations are not binding but entail a moral obligation. Increasingly, equal access to palliative care is perceived as the moral obligation of societies and governments. An active and proactive approach to palliative care can bring about, if not a revolution, then at least a radical evolution in member states.

The recommendation, being addressed to forty-five member states and 800 million people from Gibraltar to Vladivostok, cannot be a panacea. It can, however, become an agent of change, a vehicle for including palliative care in ongoing health care reforms.

It may be particularly useful for the countries which have neglected this issue; but even for the most advanced countries a review of "policies, legislative and other measures necessary for a coherent and comprehensive national policy framework for palliative care" might prove useful.

It goes without saying that palliative care services should first be in place before there can be a meaningful public debate about euthanasia. Where they are in operation, palliative care certainly decreases the demand for physician-assisted suicide, but does not solve all the problems. There is need for an open public debate, even though the chances of reaching a consensus among all forty-five member states seem to be negligible.

Appendices

Appendix I – Some key concepts

Euthanasia

The term euthanasia comes from the Ancient Greek *eu* – good, and *thanatos* – death, therefore meaning a peaceful, painless death. It refers to procedures used in cases of terminal illness to spare the patient a protracted death or extreme pain.

In practice, euthanasia can take several forms:
- active euthanasia is the intentional administration of lethal substances with the intention of ending life, either at the patient's request or, without the patient's consent, by decision of a close relative or the medical profession;

- in assisted suicide it is the patient who ends his or her own life, aided by another person who provides the necessary information or means. The term "medically assisted suicide" is used where the patient ends his or her own life by orally or intravenously taking drugs prescribed and provided by a doctor;

- indirect euthanasia is administration of analgesics resulting in death as an unintentional side-effect;

- passive euthanasia is the withholding or withdrawal of treatment necessary to sustain life.

Palliative care

The WHO (2000) defines palliative care as "an approach which improves the quality of life of patients and their families facing life-threatening illness, through the prevention, assessment and treatment of pain and other physical, psychosocial and spiritual problems".

Appendix II – A selection of useful websites

http://www.ccne-ethique.fr/
Site of the French National Consultative Ethics Committee for Health and Life Sciences (English translation available). See in particular Opinion No. 063, "Fin de vie, arrêt de vie, euthanasie" (End of life, ending life, euthanasia).

http://www.senat.fr/
Site of the French Senate (limited English translation available). Select the heading "Europe and international", click on "Europe" then go to "Comparative legislation studies". See, notably, Study LC 109 (2002) (not available in translation) on euthanasia in seven countries, supplementing Study LC 49 (1999).

http://www.genethique.org/
Forum (in French) for debate on bioethics. Dossiers available on euthanasia and palliative care, in addition to several articles, official documents and other information on the subject.

http://www.hospice-spc-council.org.uk/
Site of an association specialising in palliative care.

http://www.euthanasia.com/
Information on euthanasia research, assisted suicide, living wills, etc. Numerous links to articles, providing worldwide coverage.

http://news.bbc.co.uk/
News and documents from the BBC. Special dossier on euthanasia.

http://www.igsl-hospiz.de
Internationale Gesellschaft für Sterbebegleitung und Lebensbeistand e.V. (IGSL).
International association for end-of-life support and palliative assistance (site in German only).

http://www.dgpalliativmedizin.de/
German Association for Palliative Medicine (some items available in English).

http://www.drze.de/themen/blickpunkt/sterbehilfe
(English translation available) Page on euthanasia from the science section of the DRZE (German Reference Centre for Ethics in the Life Sciences) website.

http://www.minbuza.nl/
Multilingual site of the Netherlands Foreign Office containing a questions and answers section setting out the government policy on euthanasia.

http://www.worldrtd.org
The World Federation of Right to Die Societies, housing 37 organisations from 23 countries. A great deal of information and many links to other sites.

Appendix III

Recommendation 1418 (1999) of the Parliamentary Assembly of the Council of Europe[1]

Protection of the human rights and dignity of the terminally ill and the dying

(Extract from the Official Gazette of the Council of Europe, 1999)

1. The vocation of the Council of Europe is to protect the dignity of all human beings and the rights which stem therefrom.

2. Medical progress, which now makes it possible to cure many previously incurable or fatal diseases, the improvement of medical techniques and the development of resuscitation techniques, which make it possible to prolong a person's survival, to defer the moment of death. As a result the quality of life of the dying is often neglected, and their loneliness and suffering ignored, as is that of their families and care-givers.

3. In 1976, in its Resolution 613, the Assembly declared that it was "convinced that what dying patients most want is to die in peace and dignity, if possible with the comfort and support of their family and friends", and added in its Recommendation 779 (1976) that "the prolongation of life should not in itself constitute the exclusive aim of medical practice, which must be concerned equally with the relief of suffering".

4. Since then, the Convention for the Protection of Human Rights and Dignity of the Human Being with regard to the Application of Biology and Medicine has formed important principles and paved the way without explicitly referring to the specific requirements of the terminally ill or dying.

5. The obligation to respect and to protect the dignity of a terminally ill or dying person derives from the inviolability of human dignity in all stages of life. This respect and protection find their expression in the provision of an appropriate environment, enabling a human being to die in dignity.

1.
Assembly debate on 25 June 1999 (24th Sitting) (see Doc. 8421, report of the Social, Health and Family Affairs Committee, rapporteur: Mrs Gatterer; and Doc. 8454, opinion of the Committee on Legal Affairs and Human Rights, rapporteur: Mr McNamara).
Text adopted by the Assembly on 25 June 1999 (24th Sitting).

6. This task has to be carried out especially for the benefit of the most vulnerable members of society, a fact demonstrated by the many experiences of suffering in the past and the present. Just as a human being begins his or her life in weakness and dependency, he or she needs protection and support when dying.

7. Fundamental rights deriving from the dignity of the terminally ill or dying person are threatened today by a variety of factors:

i. insufficient access to palliative care and good pain management;

ii. often lacking treatment of physical suffering and a failure to take into account psychological, social and spiritual needs;

iii. artificial prolongation of the dying process by either using disproportionate medical measures or by continuing treatment without a patient's consent;

iv. the lack of continuing education and psychological support for health care professionals working in palliative medicine;

v. insufficient care and support for relatives and friends of terminally ill or dying patients, which otherwise could alleviate human suffering in its various dimensions;

vi. patients' fear of losing their autonomy and becoming a burden to, and totally dependent upon, their relatives or institutions;

vii. the lack or inadequacy of a social as well as institutional environment in which someone may take leave of his or her relatives and friends peacefully;

viii. insufficient allocation of funds and resources for the care and support of the terminally ill or dying;

ix. the social discrimination inherent in weakness, dying and death.

8. The Assembly calls upon member states to provide in domestic law the necessary legal and social protection against

these specific dangers and fears which a terminally ill or dying person may be faced with in domestic law, and in particular against:

i.   dying exposed to unbearable symptoms (for example, pain, suffocation, etc.);

ii. prolongation of the dying process of a terminally ill or dying person against his or her will;

iii. dying alone and neglected;

iv. dying under the fear of being a social burden;

v.   limitation of life-sustaining treatment due to economic reasons;

vi. insufficient provision of funds and resources for adequate supportive care of the terminally ill or dying.

9.   The Assembly therefore recommends that the Committee of Ministers encourage the member states of the Council of Europe to respect and protect the dignity of terminally ill or dying persons in all respects:

a.   by recognising and protecting a terminally ill or dying person's right to comprehensive palliative care, while taking the necessary measures:

i.   to ensure that palliative care is recognised as a legal entitlement of the individual in all member states;

ii. to provide equitable access to appropriate palliative care for all terminally ill or dying persons;

iii. to ensure that relatives and friends are encouraged to accompany the terminally ill or dying and are professionally supported in their endeavours. If family and/or private networks prove to be either insufficient or overstretched, alternative or supplementary forms of professional medical care are to be provided;

iv. to provide for ambulant hospice teams and networks, to ensure that palliative care is available at home, wherever ambulant care for the terminally ill or dying may be feasible;

v.   to ensure co-operation between all those involved in the care of a terminally ill or dying person;

vi. to ensure the development and implementation of quality standards for the care of the terminally ill or dying;

vii. to ensure that, unless the patient chooses otherwise, a terminally ill or dying person will receive adequate pain relief and palliative care, even if this treatment as a side-effect may contribute to the shortening of the individual's life;

viii. to ensure that health professionals are trained and guided to provide medical, nursing and psychological care for any terminally ill or dying person in co-ordinated teamwork, according to the highest standards possible;

ix. to set up and further develop centres of research, teaching and training in the fields of palliative medicine and care as well as in interdisciplinary thanatology;

x.   to ensure that specialised palliative care units as well as hospices are established at least in larger hospitals, from which palliative medicine and care can evolve as an integral part of any medical treatment;

xi. to ensure that palliative medicine and care are firmly established in public awareness as an important goal of medicine;

b. by protecting the terminally ill or dying person's right to self-determination, while taking the necessary measures:

i.   to give effect to a terminally ill or dying person's right to truthful and comprehensive, yet compassionately delivered information on his or her health condition while respecting an individual's wish not to be informed;

ii. to enable any terminally ill or dying person to consult doctors other than his or her usual doctor;

iii. to ensure that no terminally ill or dying person is treated against his or her will while ensuring that he or she is neither influenced nor pressured by another person. Furthermore, safeguards are to be envisaged to ensure that their wishes are not formed under economic pressure;

iv. to ensure that a currently incapacitated terminally ill or dying person's advance directive or living will refusing specific medical treatments is observed. Furthermore, to ensure that criteria of validity as to the scope of instructions given in advance, as well as the nomination of proxies and the extent of their authority are defined; and to ensure that surrogate decisions by proxies based on advance personal statements of will or assumptions of will are only to be taken if the will of the person concerned has not been expressed directly in the situation or if there is no recognisable will. In this context, there must always be a clear connection to statements that were made by the person in question close in time to the decision-making situation, more precisely at the time when he or she is dying, and in an appropriate situation without exertion of pressure or mental disability. To ensure that surrogate decisions that rely on general value judgments present in society should not be admissible and that, in case of doubt, the decision must always be for life and the prolongation of life;

v. to ensure that – notwithstanding the physician's ultimate therapeutic responsibility – the expressed wishes of a terminally ill or dying person with regard to particular forms of treatment are taken into account, provided they do not violate human dignity;

vi. to ensure that in situations where an advance directive or living will does not exist, the patient's right to life is not infringed upon. A catalogue of treatments which under no condition may be withheld or withdrawn is to be defined;

c. by upholding the prohibition against intentionally taking the life of terminally ill or dying persons, while:

i. recognising that the right to life, especially with regard to a terminally ill or dying person, is guaranteed by the member states, in accordance with Article 2 of the European Convention on Human Rights which states that "no one shall be deprived of his life intentionally";

ii. recognising that a terminally ill or dying person's wish to die never constitutes any legal claim to die at the hand of another person;

iii. recognising that a terminally ill or dying person's wish to die cannot of itself constitute a legal justification to carry out actions intended to bring about death.

Appendix IV

Reply from the Council of Europe Committee of Ministers to Recommendation 1418 (1999)

(adopted on 30 October 2000, at the 728th meeting of the Ministers' Deputies)

1. The Committee of Ministers has carefully considered Parliamentary Assembly Recommendation 1418 (1999) on the protection of the human rights and dignity of the terminally ill and the dying and fully shares the Assembly's concerns in this respect. The recommendation raises highly complex problems, which the Committee of Ministers has already considered in various connections, including the 1981 European Health Committee (CDSP) report on care of the dying, the 1988 euthanasia discussions of the Ad hoc Committee of Experts on Bioethics (CAHBI), and the work leading to the adoption of the Convention on Human Rights and Biomedicine (the Bioethics Convention).

2. The Committee of Ministers notes that the Assembly asks it to "encourage the member states to respect and protect the dignity of terminally ill or dying persons in all respects", particularly stressing, first, access to care, including palliative care; second, the terminally ill or dying person's right to self-determination; and, third, the prohibition on intentionally taking the life of a terminally ill or dying person.

3. The Committee of Ministers observes that the CDSP has selected the question of palliative care for a detailed study in 2001. The CDSP intends tackling the question in the wider context of the environment in which palliative care is delivered. The study will look at questions such as over-zealous medical prolongation of life, equal access to health care for old people, professional training in palliative care and reform of medical practice in hospitals and institutions.

4. As regards terminally ill or dying people's right to self-determination, the Committee of Ministers draws attention to Article 9 of the Bioethics Convention, which reads: "The previously expressed wishes relating to a medical intervention by a

patient who is not, at the time of the intervention, in a state to express his or her wishes shall be taken into account." It should be pointed out that this wording reflects the maximum convergence of views among states which took part in drawing up the convention as regards reconciling patient self-determination and medical responsibility.

5.   With regard to the absolute prohibition on intentionally taking the life of a terminally ill or dying person, the Committee of Ministers notes that the legal position differs from one member state to another on advance refusal of certain treatments and on euthanasia. Therefore, with a view to obtaining an overview of laws and/or practices of member states with regard to the issues raised by the recommendation, the Committee of Ministers instructed the Steering Committee on Bioethics (CDBI) to gather relevant information.

6.   Furthermore, the Committee of Ministers stresses that protection of the individual's fundamental rights – including those of the ill or dying – is a matter for the member states, under the supervision, where appropriate, of the European Court of Human Rights. Consequently, the Committee of Ministers has also instructed the Steering Committee for Human Rights (CDDH) to formulate an opinion on Recommendation 1418 (1999).

Appendix V

Reply from the Council of Europe Committee of Ministers to Recommendation 1418 (1999)

(adopted on 26 March 2002, at the 790th meeting of the Ministers' Deputies)

1. The Committee of Ministers welcomes the work carried out by the Parliamentary Assembly, leading to Recommendation 1418 (1999), which addresses the particularly sensitive issues of the protection of human rights and the dignity of the terminally ill and the dying. It recalls its interim reply, adopted on 30 October 2000, informing the Assembly of the terms of reference given to the Steering Committee for Human Rights (CDDH) and the Steering Committee on Bioethics (CDBI).

2. Having closely studied the resulting information and opinion, the Committee observes that member states have varying approaches to the issues dealt with in the recommendation. There are many aspects to these issues – particularly ethical, psychological and sociological aspects – but the Committee of Ministers, committed to the respect and protection of fundamental human rights, intends to restrict itself to the one incontestable area of Council of Europe competence: human rights protection under the European Convention on Human Rights and the case-law of the European Court of Human Rights.

3. Certain issues raised by the recommendation go to the heart of the Convention, particularly regarding Articles 2 (Right to life), 3 (Prohibition of torture and inhuman or degrading treatment or punishment), and 8 (Right to respect for private and family life). Since, as yet, there is no case-law of the Court which could provide precise answers to all the questions raised in the recommendation, the Committee prefers to limit itself to the following points.

4. First, under Article 1 of the Convention, the High Contracting Parties undertake to secure to everyone within their jurisdiction the rights and freedoms defined in the Convention. This is a binding obligation for all Parties, irrespective of any

expression of will by the person concerned in this respect. Therefore, in the case of patients who are entirely incapable of self-determination, the Court has pointed out that they nevertheless remain under the protection of the Convention.[1]

5.   This must be borne in mind when considering the "right of the terminally ill or the dying to self-determination", referred to notably in paragraph 9.*b* of the recommendation. The Committee of Ministers therefore welcomes in this respect paragraph 9.*c* of the Assembly recommendation, to "encourage the member states of the Council of Europe to respect and protect the dignity of terminally ill or dying persons in all respects... by upholding the prohibition against intentionally taking the life of terminally ill or dying persons, while:

i.   recognising that the right to life, especially with regard to a terminally ill or dying person, is guaranteed by the member states, in accordance with Article 2 of the European Convention on Human Rights, which states that "no one shall be deprived of his life intentionally";

ii.   recognising that a terminally ill or dying person's wish to die never constitutes any legal claim to die at the hand of another person;

iii.   recognising that a terminally ill or dying person's wish to die cannot of itself constitute a legal justification to carry out actions intended to bring about death."

6.   There can be no derogations from the right to life other than those mentioned under Article 2 of the Convention. Apart from these cases, no one may be intentionally deprived of life,[2] as the Assembly notes in paragraph 9.*c*.i. The Court has not, however, yet had occasion to rule on the relevance of Article 2 to the proposals set out in paragraph 9.*c*.ii and iii.

7.   As regards the protection of human dignity afforded by Article 3 ("no one shall be subjected to torture or to inhuman or degrading treatment or punishment"), its requirements permit of no derogation.[3] It is true that the Court stated that "as a general rule, a measure which is a therapeutic necessity cannot be regarded as inhuman or degrading",[4] but it also

noted that the assessment of an act as ill-treatment falling within the scope of Article 3 "depends on all the circumstances of the case, such as the duration of the treatment, its physical or mental effects and, in some cases, the sex, age and state of health of the victim, etc."[5] Moreover, Article 3 includes a number of obligations for the state: "Children and other vulnerable individuals, in particular, are entitled to state protection, in the form of effective deterrence, against such serious breaches of personal integrity."[6]

8.   The right to respect for private and family life, as guaranteed by Article 8, would become relevant in some instances, but there are only very rare examples of case-law from the Strasbourg organs that could be linked to questions relating to the dignity of the sick within the scope of such a provision.[7]

9.   The dual objective of alleviating suffering whilst avoiding such violations may give rise to a wide range of national measures. The recommendation draws attention to those concerning palliative care (see notably paragraph 9.*a*). Although definitions of palliative care do exist,[8] the recommendation does not define these terms any more than it gives a definition of the concept of "pain management" mentioned in paragraph 7.i – rightly in the Committee's view, as it does not seem possible to give a uniform European definition of such very broad concepts. The Committee refers in this context to the work being carried out on palliative care by the European Health Committee.[9]

10. It follows, in the Committee of Ministers' view, that several of the proposals made by the Parliamentary Assembly to member states, in particular a greater commitment on their part to relieving human suffering, can help protect human rights and the dignity of the terminally ill and the dying, provided that the articles of the European Convention on Human Rights mentioned in this reply are respected.

11. However, in the absence of precise case-law, the question of "human rights of the terminally ill and the dying", seen from the angle of the Convention, gives rise to a series of other very complex questions of interpretation, such as:

–   the question of interplay and possible conflict between the different relevant rights and freedoms and that of the margin of appreciation of the States Parties in finding solutions aiming to reconcile these rights and freedoms;

- the question of the nature and the scope of positive obligations incumbent upon States Parties and which are linked to the effective protection of rights and freedoms provided by the Convention;

- the question of whether the relevant provisions of the Convention must be interpreted as also guaranteeing "negative rights", as the Court has ruled for certain articles of the Convention,[10] as well as the question of whether an individual can renounce the exercise of certain rights and freedoms in this context (and, if that is the case, to what extent and under which conditions).

12. With regard to legislation and practices in member states concerning the problems addressed in the recommendation, the Steering Committee on Bioethics is working on a report, in accordance with the terms of reference assigned to it by the Committee of Ministers. This report, due to be finalised in the course of 2002, will be forwarded to the Assembly in due course. The CDDH, for its part, will follow the development of these issues attentively.

13. In addition, concerning issues related to palliative care, to which the Assembly devoted an important section of its recommendation, the European Health Committee (CDSP) has prepared a study of the situation in many European countries, taking particular account of the contribution made by the Eastern and Central European Task Force on Palliative Care. The CDSP has undertaken to prepare a draft recommendation on these issues. The Committee of Ministers will be apprised of the results of this work in late 2002.

14. The Committee of Ministers wishes at this stage to inform the Assembly that the proposals contained in its Recommendation 1418 (1999) have broadly contributed to the deliberations carried out in this field. Furthermore, the Committee of Ministers welcomes the contacts established between the chairpersons of the competent sub-committee of the Assembly and the Committee of Experts on the Organisation of Palliative Care.

1. European Court of Human Rights, Herczegfalvy v. Austria, 24 September 1992, Series A No. 244, paragraph 82.

2. "(Article 2) not only safeguards the right to life but sets out the circumstances when the deprivation of life may be justified; Article 2 ranks as one of the most fundamental provisions in the Convention – indeed one which, in peacetime, admits of no derogation under Article 15. Together with Article 3 of the Convention, it also enshrines one of the basic values of the democratic societies making up the Council of Europe. As such, its provisions must be strictly construed", European Court of Human Rights, McCann and Others v. the United Kingdom, 27 September 1995, paragraph 147.

3. Herczegfalvy v. Austria, paragraph 82.

4. Ibid., the Court pointed out that it had to satisfy itself that this necessity had been convincingly shown to exist.

5. European Court of Human Rights, Ireland v. the United Kingdom, 18 January 1978.

6. European Court of Human Rights, A. v. the United Kingdom, 23 September 1998, paragraph 22. States must consequently take legislative or other measures to ensure that individuals within their jurisdiction, especially the most vulnerable - which includes the terminally ill and the dying - are not subjected to inhuman or degrading treatments. Moreover, in a case involving very exceptional circumstances, the Court pointed out that the expulsion of a patient in the terminal phase of Aids to a country where health conditions were unfavourable would constitute inhuman treatment, given that his expulsion would expose him to a real risk of dying in particularly painful circumstances; see European Court of Human Rights, D. v. the United Kingdom, 2 May 1997, *Reports* 1997-III, No. 37, paragraphs 53-54.

7. European Court of Human Rights, Herczegfalvy v. Austria, paragraph 86; European Commission of Human Rights, X. v. Austria, No. 8278, *Decisions and reports* 18, paragraphs 154 and 156 (1979) (blood test), Peters v. the Netherlands, No. 21132/93, 77-A *Decisions and reports* 75 (1994) (urine test).

8. The World Health Organisation defines palliative care as "the active total care of patients whose disease is not responsive to curative treatment. Control of pain, of other symptoms and of psychological, social and spiritual problems is paramount. The goal of the palliative care is achievement of the best possible quality of life for patients and their families" (quoted in the Parliamentary Assembly

of the Council of Europe, report on the protection of the human rights and dignity of the terminally ill and the dying, Doc. 8421, 21 May 1999, by Ms Edeltraud Gatterer).

9. This work is mentioned in the interim reply adopted by the Ministers' Deputies on 30 October 2000.

10. For example, for Articles 9 and 11 of the Convention (respectively, the freedom not to have a religion and freedom not to associate with others). (See, for example, the European Court of Human Rights, Buscarini and Others v. San Marino, 18 February 1999, paragraph 34, and European Court of Human Rights, Sigurdur Sigurjonsson v. Iceland, 30 June 1993, paragraph 35).

Appendix VI

Recommendation Rec(2003)24 of the Council of Europe Committee of Ministers on the organisation of palliative care

(adopted on 12 November 2003, at the 860th meeting of the Ministers' Deputies)

The Committee of Ministers, under the terms of Article 15.*b* of the Statute of the Council of Europe,

Considering that the aim of the Council of Europe is to achieve greater unity between its members and that this aim may be pursued, *inter alia*, by the adoption of common rules in the health field;

Recalling Article 11 of the European Social Charter on the right to health protection, and recalling that Article 3 of the Convention on Human Rights and Biomedicine (ETS No.164) requires that contracting parties provide equitable access to health care of appropriate quality, that Article 4 requests that any intervention in the health field, including research, must be carried out in accordance with relevant professional obligations and standards, and that Article 10 emphasises the right of everyone to know any information about his or her health;

Recognising that a health care system should be patient-oriented and that citizens should necessarily participate in decisions regarding their health care;

Recalling in this context the recommendation of the Committee of Ministers to member states, Recommendation No. R (2000) 5 on the development of structures for citizen and patient participation in the decision-making process affecting health care;

Convinced that the respect and protection of the dignity of a terminally ill or a dying person implies above all the provision of appropriate care in a suitable environment, enabling him or her to die with dignity;

Recalling in this context Recommendation 1418 (1999) of the Parliamentary Assembly on protection of the human rights and dignity of the terminally ill and the dying;

Further recalling Recommendation No. R (89) 13, on the organisation of multidisciplinary care for cancer patients;

Recognising that palliative care needs to be further developed in European countries;

Recalling in this respect the 1998 Poznan Declaration on palliative care in Eastern Europe;

Recognising that the right to health care is aimed at the patient's enjoyment of the highest attainable sense of well-being, irrespective of age, ethnicity, economic or social status, and the nature of any disease or infirmity;

Considering that there is a growing number of people in need of palliative care;

Considering that the differences in the availability and quality of palliative care throughout Europe need to be addressed through increased co-operation between countries;

Conscious that palliative care is the active, total care of patients with advanced, progressive diseases, aiming at the control of pain and other symptoms, and offering psychological, social, and spiritual support;

Aware that the goal of palliative care is the achievement of the best possible quality of life for patients and their families;

Aware that palliative care aims to help men, women and children with advanced, progressive diseases to enjoy the best possible quality of life until the end, and intends neither to hasten nor postpone death;

Considering that palliative care affirms life and regards dying as a normal process, and is not guided by hopelessness or fatalism;

Considering that palliative care is an integral part of the health care system and an inalienable element of a citizen's right to health care, and that therefore it is a responsibility of the government to guarantee that palliative care is available to all who need it;

Considering that it is necessary to pursue the development of quality care, carried out humanely, in order to make it an essential part of health care for patients near the end of life;

Recognising that all people near the end of life desire to be treated as valued persons by health care professionals and to have skilled attention directed at maintaining dignity and fostering independence, relieving symptoms and maximising comfort;

Recognising that palliative care, like all medical care, should be patient-oriented, guided by the needs of the patient, taking into account his or her values and preferences, and that dignity and autonomy are central issues for patients in need of palliative care,

Recommends that the governments of member states:

1. adopt policies, legislative and other measures necessary for a coherent and comprehensive national policy framework for palliative care;

2. take to this end, whenever feasible, the measures presented in the appendix to this recommendation, taking account of their respective national circumstances;

3. promote international networking between organisations, research institutions and other agencies that are active in the palliative care field;

4. support an active, targeted dissemination of this recommendation and its explanatory memorandum, where appropriate accompanied by a translation.

Appendix to Recommendation Rec(2003)24

General considerations

While in many countries the greater part of health care budgets is spent on people in their final years of life, they do not always receive the care that is most appropriate to their needs.

Palliative care does not address a specific disease and spans the period from the diagnosis of advanced disease until the end of bereavement; this may vary from years to weeks or (rarely) days. It is not synonymous with terminal care, but encompasses it.

The creation, in member states, of a climate in which the importance of palliative care is recognised is crucial.

The public, including patients and their families, needs to be educated regarding the importance of palliative care, and of what it can offer.

Several recent studies, providing data in a total of thirty-five countries across Europe, have pointed out differences between countries with regard to palliative care, among which are variations in reimbursement (where applicable), in health care system organisation and in the place of palliative care within it; differing ethical and cultural factors; the role of national organisations, and international collaboration in palliative care development; opioid availability; and questions of workforce training and development.

I. *Guiding principles*

Palliative care policies should be based on values propounded by the Council of Europe: human rights and patients' rights, human dignity, social cohesion, democracy, equity, solidarity, equal gender opportunities, participation and freedom of choice.

Palliative care has the following core dimensions:

– symptom control;

– psychological, spiritual, and emotional support;

– support for the family;

– bereavement support.

The following principles underpin the recommendation:

1. Palliative care is a vital and integral part of health services. Provisions for its development and functional integration should be incorporated into national health strategies.

2. Any person who is in need of palliative care should be able to access it without undue delay, in a setting which is, as far as reasonably feasible, consistent with his or her needs and preferences.

3. Palliative care has as its objective the achievement and maintenance of the best possible quality of life for patients.

4. Palliative care seeks to address physical, psychological and spiritual issues associated with advanced disease. Therefore, it requires a co-ordinated input from a highly-skilled and adequately resourced interdisciplinary and multi-professional team.

5. Acute intervening problems should be treated if the patient so wishes, but should be left untreated, while the best palliative care continues to be provided, if the patient prefers.

6. Access to palliative care should be based on need, and must not be influenced by disease type, geographical location, socio-economic status or other such factors.

7. Programmes of palliative care education should be incorporated into the training of all concerned health care professionals.

8. Research aimed at improving the quality of care should be undertaken. All palliative care interventions should be supported to the greatest possible extent by relevant research data.

9. Palliative care should receive an adequate and equitable level of funding.

10. As in all sectors of medical care, health care providers involved in palliative care should fully respect patients' rights,

comply with professional obligations and standards, and, in that context, act in the best interest of the patients.

II. Settings and services

1. Palliative care is an interdisciplinary and multi-professional undertaking which attends to the needs of the patient, while not neglecting the informal caregivers, such as family members.

2. Palliative care services and policies must offer a wide range of resources, such as home care, in-patient care in specific or conventional units, day hospital and out-patient clinics, emergency call-out and respite care facilities. These should be comprehensive and appropriate to the health care system and culture, and should focus on the changing needs and wishes of patients.

3. Informal caregivers should be supported in their caregiving, and should not incur major social setbacks, such as job loss, as a consequence of caregiving. A formal right to "care leave" may be desirable.

4. All professionals involved in the care of patients with advanced, progressive disease should have easy access to specific expertise if and when they need it.

5. Specialist palliative care should be available for all patients when they need it, at any time and in any situation.

6. It should be ensured that there is leadership in the development of palliative care at national level and proper coordination of services with a clear allocation of responsibilities. The formation of regional networks is recommended as a good means to reach this goal.

7. Patients should be guaranteed access to palliative care without undue financial barriers. Financial and other arrangements should be such that continuity in palliative care is guaranteed, and is adapted to the needs of the patient.

8. There should be sufficient respite care facilities to offer temporary relief when caregivers in the home become overburdened.

III. *Policy and organisation*

1. Palliative care must be an integral part of a country's health care system, and as such it must be an element of comprehensive health care plans, and of specific programmes concerning, for instance, cancer, Aids or geriatrics.

2. Governments should have a needs assessment study performed that addresses the need for services, for personnel of different levels of expertise, and for training of different professions (including volunteers).

3. On the basis of a needs assessment, national or regional governments need to design and implement comprehensive rational palliative care strategies in close collaboration with professionals and patients and families, or their representatives.

4. As part of such strategies, governments should identify legal, social, economic, cultural, administrative and/or physical barriers in access to palliative care services. Initiatives and programmes should be implemented in order to reduce such barriers, which often lead to inequalities.

5. Legislation should make opioids and other drugs accessible in a range of formulations and dosages for medical use. The fear of abuse should not hinder access to necessary and effective medication. Countries may wish to consider whether this will require new legislation or an amendment to existing legislation.

6. It is recommended that, both at national and at regional and local level, interdisciplinary focal groups or councils devoted to palliative care involving patients, families and others be constituted in order to maintain political and social attention. Preferably, such groups co-operate with governments and other bodies in putting in place the necessary policies.

7. In order to facilitate the monitoring of the quality of palliative care, the constitution of a uniform "minimum data set" (MDS) is necessary, at least at national level.

8. Because of the importance of equity, special attention should be paid to palliative care for underprivileged groups (for instance, prisoners those with learning disabilities, the

homeless, refugees) and to cultural and ethnic differences related to the needs of patients. Equally importantly, special attention should be paid to palliative care for children.

9. Professional caregivers are entitled to a fair remuneration, and to recognition for the work they do and for their competence.

10. A national annual report on organisation and functioning of palliative care should be published.

IV. *Quality improvement and research*

1. The definition and adoption of indicators of good palliative care assessing all dimensions of care from the perspective of the patient should be encouraged.

2. Clinical practice guidelines for palliative care, based on the best available evidence, should be developed in a systematic way, with the participation of patients.

3. Continuous feedback on practices in the form of an audit is essential to quality control.

4. Even though scientific research in palliative care may pose specifically pressing ethical problems, care services and medical intervention should be evaluated using proven scientific methods, both qualitative and quantitative in nature. The focus of such studies should be patient-related.

5. Collaborative research, both at national and at European level, should be encouraged.

6. An observatory should be set up at national and regional level to collect, process and disseminate reliable information on developments in and quality of palliative care.

V. *Education and training*

1. Both for research and for education, academic recognition of palliative care is important.

2. Palliative care should be included in all undergraduate training of doctors and nurses. Standard curricula should be established, as well as postgraduate training and education,

and there should be training programmes for experts in palliative care.

3. International co-operation on education should be encouraged, for example by establishing a directory of palliative care units wishing to participate in twinning programmes.

4. All professionals and non-professionals involved in palliative care should be trained appropriately for their task; they should receive at all levels of training concrete, insightful and culturally sensitive instruction in palliative care.

5. Education in palliative care should be both monodisciplinary and interdisciplinary.

6. Education in palliative care should be regularly followed up, for instance in the form of supervision.

7. Centres of reference should be set up in each country for teaching and training in palliative care.

8. Ideally, there should be the following three levels of (continuing) education for professionals: basic, intermediary and advanced education.

9. It is recommended that countries devote specific attention to educating the general public about all relevant aspects of palliative care.

10. The unjustified negative images concerning opioids among patients, families, professionals and the public should be corrected, with the essential differences between the clinical applications and the potential for abuse being stressed, both in public campaigns and professional education.

VI. *The family*

1. The aim and the principle, in helping those close to patients (principally family members), are to put to good use and to develop their ability to bring emotional and practical support to patients, to adapt to the process, and to cope with grief and loss. Particular attention must be paid to the prevention of and the treatment of depression from exhaustion.

VII. *Communication with patient and family*

1. Palliative care demands a climate, an attitude and a caregiver-patient relationship which encourage openness in information to patients and families.

2. Professionals should take into account the extent to which patients wish to be informed about their situation; in this regard, attention should be paid to cultural differences.

3. Professionals should adapt the way in which they give information to patients to the emotional or cognitive barriers that are often associated with having an advanced and progressive illness.

4. Where children are involved, either because of their own illness or because of the illness of a parent, communication should be adapted to their needs.

VIII. *Teams, teamwork and care planning*

1. Palliative care is an interdisciplinary and multiprofessional undertaking, most often involving a physician and a nurse and other health care workers who have the expertise needed to respond to the physical, psychological, and spiritual needs of the patient and the family. The functioning of such teams should be facilitated.

2. Decision-making, especially the making, monitoring and regular reviewing of individual anticipatory care plans, should be shared between the patient, the family and the team, whenever this is appropriate, and complies fully with the patients' wishes. Appropriate communication between the various services involved (curative and palliative) should be ensured.

3. Volunteers can be an important part of the team. They do not take over the work of professionals, but have their own contribution and expertise. The setting-up of volunteer services, and the process of becoming a volunteer, should be facilitated.

4. All team members should be competent in their roles and aware of the possibilities and limitations of both their own role and that of the other members.

5. Receiving coherent messages from different care providers is crucial for the patient and the family. Therefore, optimal information flows between care providers are essential in order to avoid misunderstandings or discrepancies. It is advisable to establish a leading co-ordinator, preferably, depending on circumstances, the primary physician.

6. All communication between professionals concerning patients and families is subject to professional secrecy, fully respecting the patient's right to medical secrecy and the families' right to privacy.

7. Palliative care is usually very rewarding, but equally it can be very demanding. Therefore, caring for the caregivers is an essential part of palliative care, and the occupational health of those working in palliative care should be a focus of policies.

IX. *Bereavement*

1. Bereavement care services should be offered to those who are in need of support.

2. All professional workers in palliative care should be attentive to signs of complicated or disturbed bereavement.